Integrated Science

for Jamaica

Grade 7 Workbook

Fourth Edition

Tania Chung

macmillan education

Macmillan Education
4 Crinan Street
London N1 9XW
A division of Springer Nature Limited

Companies and representatives throughout the world

ISBN 978-1-380-02336-0

Third edition published 2007
This edition published 2019

Designed by Macmillan Education
Page make-up, typesetting and illustration by TechType
Cover design by Macmillan Education
Cover photograph by Tiffany Lue-Yen

The publishers would like to thank Tanya Murray for advising.

Printed and bound in Italy
2022 2021 2020 2019
10 9 8 7 6 5 4 3 2

Integrated Science for Jamaica Grade 7 Workbook

Contents

UNIT 1 Working like a scientist

Multiple choice questions

Circle the letter that *best* corresponds to the answer of your choice.

1 Which statement *best* describes a scientist?

a a person who only likes to ask questions

b a curious person who likes to find out answers to questions

c a person who uses a lot of chemicals

d none of the above

2 Which of the following is **not** a fundamental quantity?

a length

b mass

c volume

d time

3 What is the name of the piece of apparatus drawn below?

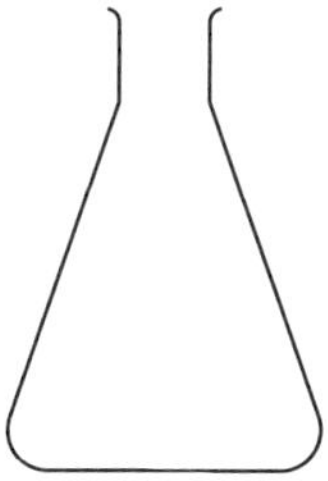

a beaker

b evaporating dish

c measuring cylinder

d conical flask

4 Theodore is a first-form student visiting the school laboratory for the first time. Which of the following is **not** a rule to follow while working in the laboratory?

a keep your work area clean and uncluttered at all times

b use all your five senses to observe substances used in experiments

c report all accidents in the laboratory to your science teacher

d only enter the laboratory when given permission by a teacher

5 Identify the safety symbol you are most likely to see on a packet of pesticide.

a 

b 

c 

d 

6 Which safety symbol would you expect to see on a bottle of methylated spirits?

a 

b 

c 

d 

7 Which of the following senses should you *never* use in the laboratory, unless instructed to do so by a teacher?

a sight
b touch
c taste
d smell

8 Which sense organ is responsible for touch?

a fingers
b skin
c tongue
d hands

9 Identify the missing step in the engineering design process:

problem → ____________ → specify requirements → generate solutions → build prototype → test and redesign → communicate results

a solution
b research
c make
d engineer

10 What instrument is used to measure the volume of a liquid?

a measuring tape
b measuring cylinder
c metre rule
d thermometer

11 Use the correct instrument to measure the length of the line below and circle the correct length.

____

a 24 cm
b 2.5 cm
c 25 cm
d 2.4 cm

12 What is the volume of liquid in this measuring cylinder?

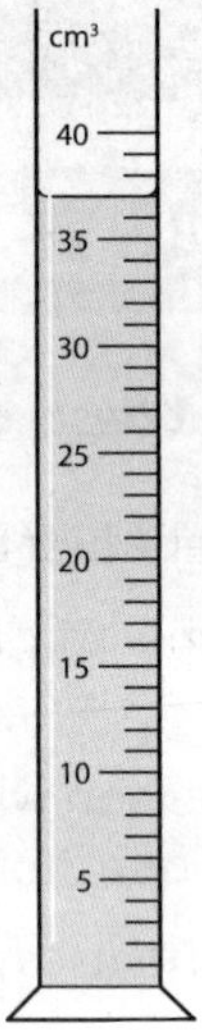

a 36.5 cm^3
b 35.2 cm^3
c 37 cm^3
d 30.7 cm^3

13 Which sentence best describes the steps John should take when smelling a chemical in the laboratory?

a he should put his nose over the chemical and inhale strongly
b he should put his nose over the chemical and exhale strongly
c he should fan vapours to his nose and inhale gently
d he should fan vapours to his nose and inhale strongly

14 What instrument is used to measure temperature?

a mercury
b fingers
c barometer
d thermometer

15 Which sentence best defines the word *science*?

- **a** the study of chemicals
- **b** the study of living things only
- **c** the study of living and non-living things
- **d** the study of non-living things only

16 What is the curved surface of a liquid in a container called?

- **a** curvature
- **b** meniscus
- **c** dent
- **d** trough

17 What colour code is used on the labels of safety symbols found on dangerous substances?

- **a** yellow
- **b** red
- **c** orange
- **d** black

18 Define *technology*.

- **a** using robots to help us
- **b** the application of science to improve the quality of life
- **c** anything that is powered by electricity
- **d** engineering

19 Which of the following statements about graphs is correct.

- **a** the *x*-axis is the horizontal axis
- **b** the *x*-axis is the vertical axis
- **c** the *x*-axis can be the horizontal or vertical axis
- **d** the *x*-axis connects the points plotted on the graph

20 Which of these is a unit of mass?

- **a** metres
- **b** grams
- **c** litres
- **d** kilometres

Use the diagram below to answer questions 21 and 22.

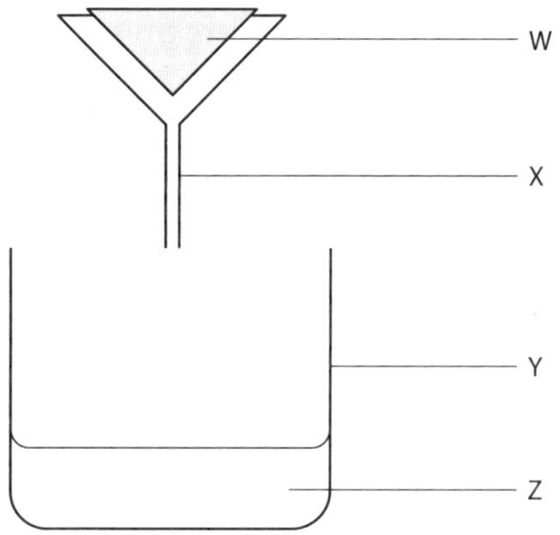

21 Look at the apparatus below. Which piece of apparatus, A–D, represents a beaker?

a W **b** X **c** Y **d** Z

22 Which piece of apparatus, A–D, functions as a sieve (strainer)?

a W **b** X **c** Y **d** Z

23 The first step in the scientific method is a *problem*. What is the first step in the engineering design process?

- **a** research
- **b** problem
- **c** design
- **d** make

24 Which of the following guidelines should you follow when making a scientific drawing?

- **a** use a very sharp pencil
- **b** make sure that lines are clean, even and continuous
- **c** label lines must be straight and not crossed
- **d** all of the above

25 Identify the Jamaican scientist who extracted a chemical from cannabis which is used for the treatment of a rare cancer called *acute myeloid leukaemia.*

a Dr. Henry Lowe

b Prof. Manley West

c Dr. Lawrence Williams

d Dr. Paula Tennant

26 Which of the following is **not** a unit of volume?

a cubic centimetres

b litres

c millilitres

d centimetres

27 How many seconds are there in one hour?

a 60 **b** 360

c 3,600 **d** 120

28 Identify the correct instrument and unit for measuring electric current.

a instrument = ammeter; unit = volts

b instrument = voltmeter; unit = volts

c instrument = voltmeter; unit = amperes

d instrument = ammeter; unit = amperes

29 A student selects a leaf of length 6.2 cm to draw. Her drawing is 15.5 cm in length. What is the magnification of the drawing?

a ×0.4 **b** ×96.1

c ×2.5 **d** ×21.7

30 Complete this sentence: The amount of matter that an object contains is known as its…

a …volume **b** …weight

c …mass **d** …length

Structured questions

Write your answers in the spaces provided.

1 A stone was placed on a balance.
Diagram A shows the reading on the scale of the balance.

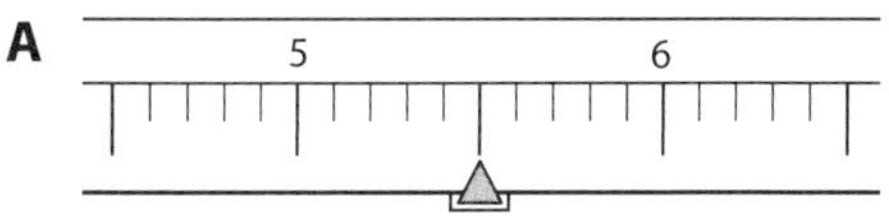

a Write down the mass of the stone. Mass of stone = ___ g.

The stone was then placed into a measuring cylinder.

Diagram B shows the volume of water before the stone was placed into it.

Diagram C shows the volume of the water after the stone was placed into it.

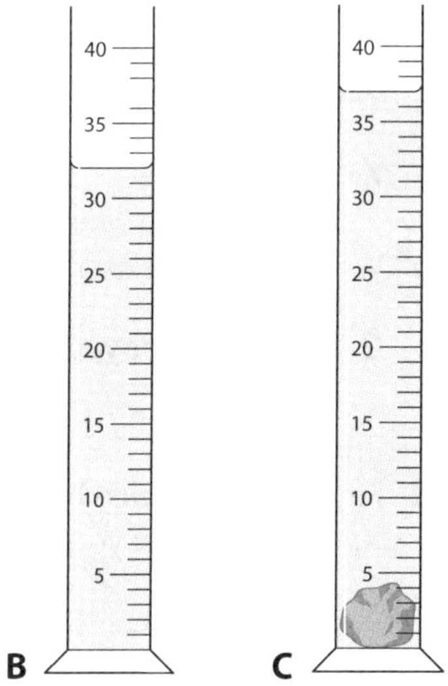

b Complete the calculation to find the density of the stone:

initial volume = ___ cm^3

final volume = ___ cm^3

volume of stone = final volume – initial volume = ___ cm^3

density of stone = $\frac{\text{mass of stone}}{\text{volume of stone}}$ = ___ g/cm

2 Complete this table by adding the use of each instrument.

Instrument	Use
Ammeter	
Stethoscope	
Binoculars	
Gieger counter	
Metre rule	

3 Look at this image, then answer the questions that follow.

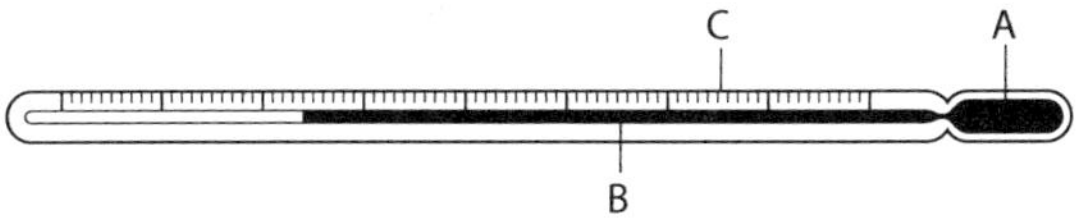

a What is the name of the apparatus? ______________________

b Label structures A–C.

A ______________ B ______________ C ______________

4 This image shows sections of three thermometers.

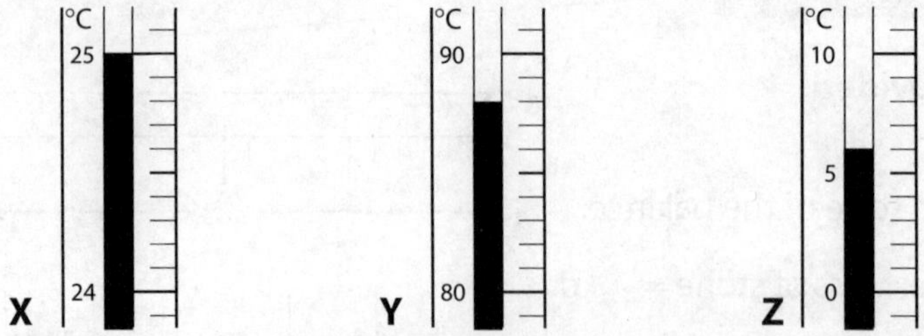

a What is the temperature reading on each thermometer?

X ________ °C **Y** ________ °C **Z** ________ °C

b Which thermometer, X, Y or Z, has just been inserted in a hot liquid? ____________

c Give a reason for your answer.

____

d Find the difference between the highest and lowest temperature on the thermometers X, Y and Z. Show your working.

____

____

5 Mary made a box using measurements that were four times bigger than those shown in the drawing, right.

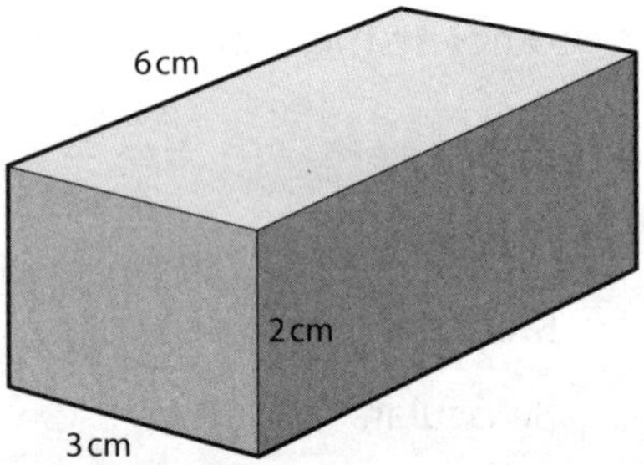

a What are the dimensions of Mary's box?

Length = ________ cm

Width = ________ cm

Height = ________ cm

b What is the volume of the box that Mary made? Show your working.

____

____

c The centimetre (cm) is a unit from the International System of Units, or metric system. As a scientist, why do you think it is important that we use the metric system?

____

____

____

6 A student from your science class placed two bungs in a trough of water. One bung sank and the other floated.

a Following the scientific method, identify the *problem* that you would want to investigate.

____

____

b What is a *hypothesis*?

____

____

C Write a hypothesis based on your answer to question **a**

____

____

7 Look at this picture of children playing, then answer the questions that follow.

a Identify **three** possible accidents that could happen.

____

____

____

b Write **four** safety rules for this playground.

____

____

____

____

8 Look at this picture of students working in a science laboratory, then answer the questions that follow.

a Identify **three** accidents that may happen in this laboratory.

---

b Write **four** rules for the students in this laboratory to ensure safety.

---

c Create a safety sign outlining **two** safety apparel that should be worn by students working in the laboratory.

Investigative comprehension

Read the comprehension passage and answer the questions that follow.

Do green leaves contain starch?

Vaughn learned that green plants make their own food (glucose) by a process called photosynthesis. Some of the glucose is converted to starch and other molecules used by the plant.

Vaughn decided to investigate whether green leaves contain starch. He picked a green hibiscus leaf. He examined the leaf and used a ruler to measure its length. He then drew and labelled a diagram of the leaf. He labelled the apex, lamina, midrib, margin, veins, and petiole. He completed his diagram by writing a title and the magnification. He calculated the magnification by dividing the length of the drawing by the length of the actual leaf.

After completing his drawing, Vaughn carried out an experiment to investigate whether the green leaf contains starch. He first placed the green leaf in hot water for two minutes to stop all chemical reactions by 'killing' the leaf. The leaf was then placed in a boiling tube containing ethanol which he placed in a water bath at 85 °C. This was a safety precaution to ensure that there wasn't an open flame to ignite the ethanol (a highly flammable substance). After a few minutes, he noticed that the leaf lost its colour (became decolourised) and the ethanol liquid became green.

Vaughn removed the decolourised leaf, washed it in warm water, and placed it on a white tile. He then added a few drops of iodine to the leaf. The leaf became blue-black.

1 Write a hypothesis for the investigation carried out by Vaughn.

____

2 Pick a small green hibiscus leaf from a plant outside and tape it in the box below.

a Measure and record the length of the green hibiscus leaf.

Length of leaf = ____ cm

b Describe the hibiscus leaf.

____

____

c Draw and label a diagram of your hibiscus leaf on a sheet of paper. Use the same labels as Vaughn did. Make sure you apply the proper criteria for a scientific drawing. Fold and stick your picture in the space below.

d Measure the length of your drawing. Length of drawing = ____ cm

e Calculate the magnification of your drawing.

____

3 Why did Vaughn make a scientific drawing?

____

____

4 Why was it important for Vaughn to use a ruler to measure the leaf, and not just his eyes?

____

5 Write a conclusion for Vaughn's experiment.

____

____

6 Gardener's and farmers will often use pesticides when cultivating flowers. What risks are associated with using these chemicals?

____

____

____

True or false?

State whether each statement is true or false.

1 Professor Errol Morris has worked on a cure for asthma. ____________

2 We use a Bunsen burner to provide heat in the laboratory. ____________

3 Students should be allowed in a laboratory unsupervised. ____________

4 A thermometer is an instrument used to measure mass. ____________

5 We should smell all chemicals used in the laboratory. ____________

6 A microscope helps us to see large things smaller. ____________

7 The litre is a unit of volume. ____________

8 We use our senses when making observations. ____________

9 The horizontal axis on a graph is called the y-axis. ____________

10 The scientific method is a systematic way of carrying out an investigation. ____________

What am I?

Write the name of who or what the statement refers to.

1 Can be given in units of metres, centimetres or millimetres. ____________

2 The unit for volume. ____________

3 Used to measure exactly how hot or cold a substance is. ____________

4 An ancient instrument used to tell time. ____________

5 The curved surface of liquids in a container. ____________

6 Used to detect the human heartbeat. ____________

7 The receptors that give humans the sense of taste when they eat food. ____________

8 Posted in gas stations to remind you of the dangers of gasoline. ____________

Matching

Draw lines to connect the scientist with their field of science.

Scientist
marine biologist
botanist
zoologist
hydrologist
ecologist

Field of study
studies animals and animal life
studies the sea and its interaction with organisms living in it
studies water and water systems
studies the relationship between living things and their environment
studies plants

Fill in the blanks

Complete the passage using the words below. Some words can be used once, more than once or not at all.

colourless mercury thermometer Celsius dye alcohol
temperature hazard stem liquid visible bulb

The instrument used for measuring temperature is called a ______________________.

______________________ can be measured in degrees ______________________ (°C).

The liquid used inside a thermometer is either ______________________ or ______________________.

Most of the liquid used in the thermometer is contained in the ______________________.
A small amount goes up a tiny tube inside the ______________________.

Developing a scientific mind

1 Write a poem or song about measurement. Remember to include the instruments and units used for each quantity you mention. Share it with your class.

2 Construct a large, model thermometer from cardboard and coloured paper. Ensure that the alcohol band can move to show changes in temperature. Be creative in choosing suitable materials and stick a photo of your model in the space below.

Hidden message word search

What is the hidden message? Complete the word search by circling the words in the list that are hidden in the puzzle. Then find the hidden message in the word puzzle, by recording all the letters that have not been circled, moving from left to right of each row, starting with the first row.

S	R	S	R	P	S	L	H	S	Y	E	G	E	S	V
U	M	E	O	O	E	E	C	M	R	N	R	C	I	O
C	Y	A	T	N	T	I	N	U	O	U	N	N	S	L
S	O	T	G	E	E	P	T	S	T	M	E	E	E	U
I	T	T	E	N	M	A	E	L	E	E	T	I	H	M
N	H	O	T	F	R	O	U	C	N	S	E	C	T	E
E	B	I	N	E	A	C	M	I	E	R	I	S	O	S
M	S	E	P	G	I	S	R	R	A	R	N	I	P	N
T	A	M	A	R	U	A	M	M	E	T	E	R	Y	S
T	E	S	G	K	M	E	R	U	M	H	E	N	H	N
T	T	A	S	F	E	O	R	M	E	A	T	S	I	U
R	T	N	E	M	E	R	U	S	A	E	M	K	I	N
N	O	I	T	A	V	R	E	S	B	O	S	G	B	L
E	Y	E	S	O	C	O	N	C	L	U	S	I	O	N
R	U	L	E	R	O	D	P	R	E	S	S	U	R	E

AGRICULTURE AMMETER BEAKER CONCLUSION EYES HYPOTHESIS LENGTH MARINE
MASS MEASUREMENT MENISCUS NOSE OBSERVATION RECEPTOR RULER SAFETY
SCIENCE SCIENTIST SENSES SKIN TEMPERATURE THERMOMETER TONGUE VOLUME

The hidden message:

A _

_ _

UNIT 2 Matter

Multiple choice questions

Circle the letter that *best* corresponds to the answer of your choice.

1 Which statement best describes the term *matter*?

- **a** anything that has mass but does not take up space
- **b** made up of solids
- **c** anything that takes up space
- **d** anything that has mass and takes up space

2 The characteristics of two unknown substances, X and Y, are given below.

X takes the shape of its container.

Y takes the shape of its container and the particles move freely to take the volume of the container.

Which option is correct for both X *and* Y?

- **a** X = gas; Y = solid
- **b** X = gas; Y = liquid
- **c** X = liquid; Y = solid
- **d** X = liquid; Y = gas

3 When water is heated, it rapidly changes into steam. What is this process called?

- **a** boiling
- **b** condensation
- **c** melting
- **d** evaporation

4 Which of the following is a *state of matter*?

- **a** solid
- **b** gas
- **c** liquid
- **d** all of the above

5 Which of the following properties are **not** true for solids?

- **a** particles are far apart
- **b** they have a definite shape
- **c** cannot be compressed
- **d** particles can only vibrate in a fixed position

6 In which state of matter is ice?

- **a** liquid
- **b** plasma
- **c** solid
- **d** gas

7 Identify the scientist who discovered the state of matter known as *plasma*.

- **a** Benjamin Franklin
- **b** William Crooks
- **c** Lawrence Williams
- **d** Albert Einstein

8 Which statement best describes a *chemical change*?

- **a** a reaction in which no new substance is formed
- **b** a reaction in which a new substance is formed
- **c** a reversible reaction
- **d** a reaction that involves a change of state

9 What percentage of the Earth's surface is covered with water?

a 0.5% **b** 70%
c 95% **d** 30%

10 Complete this sentence: Clouds are formed by the process of…

a …condensation
b …evaporation
c …sublimation
d …breeze

11 Claire conducted an experiment in which she heated a black solid, which turned into a purple gas. What is the black solid most likely to be?

a calcium carbonate
b iodine
c ammonium chloride
d dried ice

12 In Claire's experiment, what type of change occurred?

a boiling **b** sublimation
c melting **d** freezing

13 Which of these substances will have particles with the most energy?

a wood **b** oxygen
c glucose solution **d** rain water

14 Identify the statement that best defines *evaporation*.

a solids changing to a liquid when heated
b liquids changing to a solid when cooled
c liquids changing to a gas when heated
d liquids changing to a gas when cooled

15 This diagram shows the water cycle.

Select the option that correctly labels the processes at X, Y and Z.

a X = condensation; Y = transpiration; Z = evaporation
b X = precipitation; Y = evaporation; Z = condensation
c X = evaporation; Y = condensation; Z = transpiration
d X = evaporation; Y = condensation; Z = precipitation

16 Which step in the water cycle leads to rainfall?

a evaporation
b condensation
c precipitation
d transpiration

17 Complete this sentence: Solids have a fixed shape because the…

a …particles vibrate uniformly
b …particles are closely packed in an orderly fashion
c …particles are free to move around
d …inter-particle force is weak

18 Identify the solid that will sublime when heated.

a dry ice **b** salt
c limestone **d** ice

19 Name the process by which iodine vapours return to the solid state when cooled.

a sublimation **b** condensation
c evaporation **d** deposition

20 What happens to wax when it is heated?

a melts **b** condenses
c evaporates **d** freezes

21 Which of these changes is an example of a physical change?

a crushing a lump of chalk
b exposing hydrogen peroxide to sunlight
c frying an egg
d baking a cake

22 Identify the substance that is an example of matter.

a ice **b** gold
c wool **d** all of the above

23 Which diagram best illustrates the arrangement of the particles in a gas?

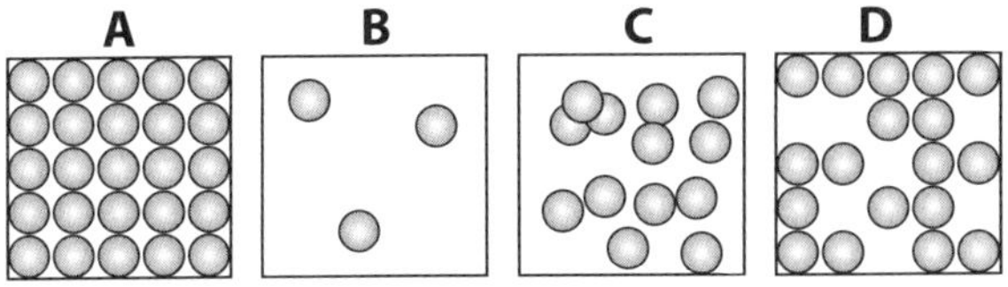

a A **b** B **c** C **d** D

24 Which of these substances will take the shape *and* volume of its container?

a water **b** ice
c carbon dioxide **d** glass

25 You are provided with four blocks made from different materials. They are all identical in size. Which block is likely to be most dense?

a plastic **b** iron
c wooden **d** glass

26 Which of these temperatures would cause the fastest movement of particles in liquid or gases?

a 0 °C **b** 32 °C **c** 78 °C **d** 100 °C

27 Identify the **false** statement about metals.

a heat can be transferred through metals
b metals will expand when heated
c metals can expand and fill the volume of their containers at room temperature
d the particles of metals at room temperature have very little energy

28 Which of the following are difficult to compress?

a water **b** steam
c ice **d** none of the above

29 At what temperature does water freeze?

a 0 °C **b** 32 °C **c** 78 °C **d** 100 °C

30 Complete this sentence: When the solid naphthalene is heated, it will…

a …freeze **b** …sublime
c …condense **d** …melt

Structured questions

Write your answers in the spaces provided.

1 a State the difference between a physical change and a chemical change.

____

b State whether the following changes are physical or chemical changes.

Dissolving sugar: ______________ Frying an egg: ______________

Melting wax: ______________ Burning a piece of paper: ______________

Baking a cake: ______________ Shredding paper: ______________

c Use the two equations below to answer the questions that follow.

Reaction A

$$\text{ice} \underset{(y)}{\overset{(x)}{\rightleftharpoons}} \text{water}$$

Reaction B

$$\text{carbon} + \text{oxygen} \rightarrow \text{carbon dioxide}$$

I What is the difference in the reaction arrows used in Reaction A and Reaction B?

____

____

II What processes are occurring at (x) and (y) in Reaction A?

____

____

III Which of the processes occurring at (x) and (y) would involve reducing the energy of the particles?

____

2 Look at this change of state diagram:

a Write the processes involved at A–D.

A ______________

B ______________

C ______________

D ______________

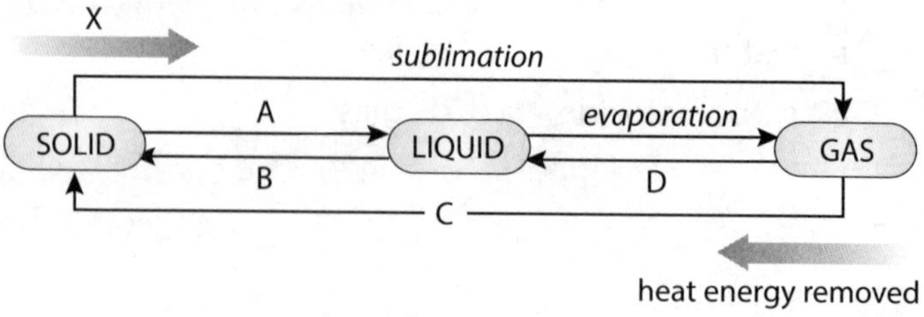

b What condition is required for a change of state in the direction of X?

___

c Name **one** substance that will undergo *sublimation*.

___

d Write a definition for the term *evaporation*.

___

___

e What would eventually happen if heat energy was continually removed from a liquid?

___

f Complete this table by recording the process that would occur for each description given.

Description	Process
Ice left in a glass on the table	
Dry ice exposed to heat	
Drying (wet) clothes in the Sun	
Cooling iodine vapours	
Water droplets forming on a pot lid during cooking	

3 Look at this diagram showing a simplified version of the water cycle.

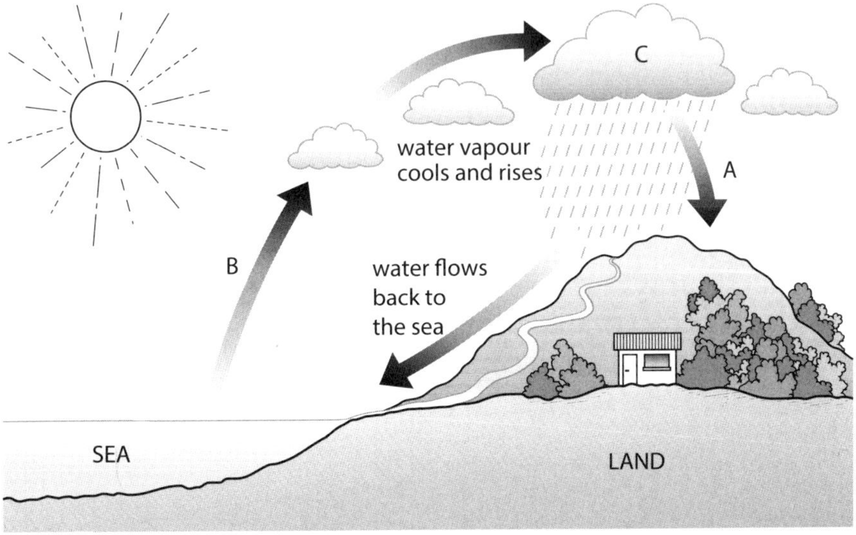

a Name the processes that occur at **A** and **B**.

A ___ **B** ___

b What is another term used for the water cycle?

___

c Explain what happens at **C**.

___

___

d Give **one** reason why the water cycle is important.

___

___

e What percentage of the Earth's surface is covered with water? ___

f Explain how trees contribute to the water cycle.

___

___

___

___

g Write a description of what happens in the water cycle.

___

___

___

___

___

Investigative comprehension

Read the comprehension passage and answer the questions that follow.

The water cycle

Christopher learned about the water cycle in his science class. He found out that when heat is applied to ice, it **melts** to form water. If heated further, it **evaporates** to form steam. When the steam is cooled, it **condenses** back into water and, if cooled further, it **freezes** to become ice. These are examples of physical changes, which means that the reactions are reversible.

Christopher also learned that plants lose water through their leaves by the process of **transpiration** and that the water evaporates into the atmosphere. So, he decided to conduct an investigation to find out how much water is lost by a leaf on three different plants over a period of 48 hours.

He selected three plants for his investigation, all from the same environment and roughly the same size. He labelled them A, B and C.

He tied a transparent, colourless plastic bag over one leaf on each plant. After a few hours, he noticed that the bags looked foggy; he could see condensation on the inner surface of the bag. After 48 hours, Christopher emptied the liquid that had collected into separate measuring cylinders and recorded the volumes. These diagrams show the volume of liquid collected for each plant.

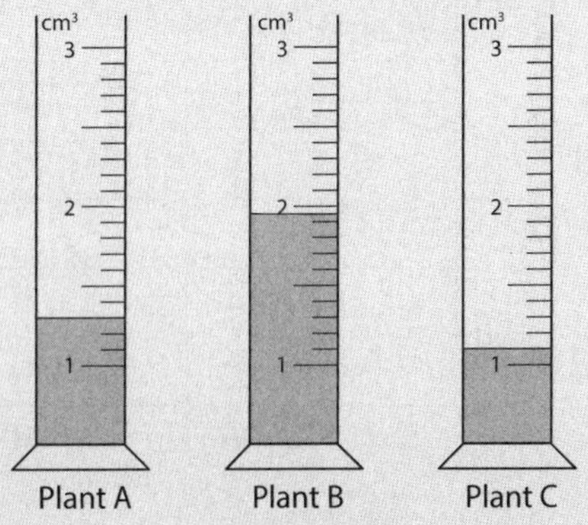

Christopher then tested the samples of liquid with blue anhydrous cobalt(II) chloride. In all cases, it changed from blue to pink. This was a positive test for the presence of water.

1 Which process in the water cycle leads to the purification of water? Explain your answer.

2 Write an aim and hypothesis for Christopher's experiment.

3 What apparatus and materials did Christopher use in his investigation?

4 Complete this table by filling in the volumes of water collected from the leaf of each plant.

Plant	Volume of water collected (cm^3)
A	
B	
C	

5 Draw a bar graph to show Christopher's results.

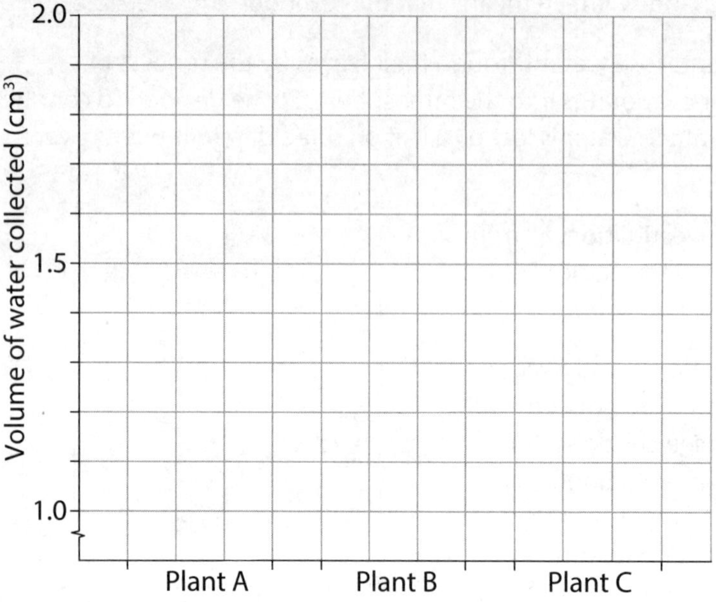

6 Name **two** conditions that Christopher kept constant for the three plants.

____

____

7 Which plant do you think had the largest leaf? Give a reason for your answer.

____

____

____

____

True or false?

State whether each statement is true or false.

1 Liquids are easily compressed. ______

2 Wax hardens when heated. ______

3 Solids take the shape of their containers. ______

4 Gases are very easy to compress. ______

5 A substance made up of one kind of atom is called a molecule. ______

6 The particles in the walls of your classroom are closely packed. ______

7 Evaporation is a physical change. ______

8 The water cycle is also known as the hydrologic cycle. ______

9 Reversible reactions result in a new product being formed. ______

10 Rain, snow and hail are examples of precipitation. ______

What am I?

Write the name of who or what the statement refers to.

1 The state in which particles are closely packed and vibrate in a fixed position. ______

2 The continuous movement of water on, above and below the Earth. ______

3 Takes the shape and fills its container. ______

4 A solid that changes to a gas that is naturally found in air. ______

5 Formed when water vapour condenses to form a collection of water droplets in the sky. ______

6 The process by which water evaporates from the leaves of plants. ______

7 Has mass and takes up space. ______

8 Has particles that can be pushed slightly closer together. ______

Matching

Draw lines to connect each process with its definition.

Process
melting
deposition
sublimation
condensation
freezing

Definition
change from liquid to solid when heat is removed
change from solid to liquid when heat is applied
change from gas to liquid when heat is removed
change from a solid directly into a gas when heat is applied
change from a gas directly to a solid on cooling

Fill in the blanks

Complete the passage using the words below. Some words can be used once, more than once or not at all.

states substances liquid closely energy particles
matter space force elements vibrate combine random

The particles of matter fit together in different ways to form different ________________.

The ________________ of solids are ________________ packed and they can only ________________ in a fixed position. Their particles are held together by a strong ________________.

Liquid particles flow past each other and move in a ________________ motion.

The ________________ of gases have a lot of ________________ and move around quickly. Gas particles will move to fill the available ________________.

Developing a scientific mind

Physical or chemical change?

You will need:

- transparent glass bowl/cup
- tablespoon baking soda
- vinegar, measuring cup

Method

1 Place two tablespoons of baking soda in the bowl.

2 Add $\frac{1}{2}$ cup of vinegar (which is an acid).

1 Describe the baking soda (include state, colour and texture).

____

2 Record what you observed when the two chemicals were added together.

____

3 What did you observe to indicate that a gas was produced?

____

4 Did this activity demonstrate a physical or chemical change? Give a reason for your answer.

____

5 Research online to help you answer the following questions

a Find out the name and chemical formula of the active ingredient in baking soda.

____

____

b What is the name of the acid found in vinegar? ______________________________

c What is the name of the gas produced in this reaction? ______________________________

d In the laboratory, which chemical can be used to test for the gas produced in this reaction?

____

Crossword puzzle

Across

2. Physical changes are normally temporary and ________________.
4. When plants lose water by evaporation.
6. The liquid form of ice.
9. The movement of fluid (liquid or gas) particles from a region of high concentration to lower concentration.
10. Changing from a liquid to a solid on cooling.
11. Change from a gas directly to a solid when cooled.
12. Rain, hail, snow are all examples.

Down

1. Lightning is an example of this state of matter.
3. Change from a liquid to a gas when heat is applied.
5. Changing from a solid to a liquid when heat is applied.
7. Droplets of condensed water in the sky.
8. Change from a gas to a liquid when cooled.

UNIT 3 Cells and organisms

Multiple choice questions

Circle the letter that *best* corresponds to the answer of your choice.

1 Which characteristic about plant cells is **false**?

a plant cells have a large central vacuole

b plant cells have a fixed shape

c plant cells can change their shape

d plant cells have a cell membrane

2 Identify structure X in the animal cell below.

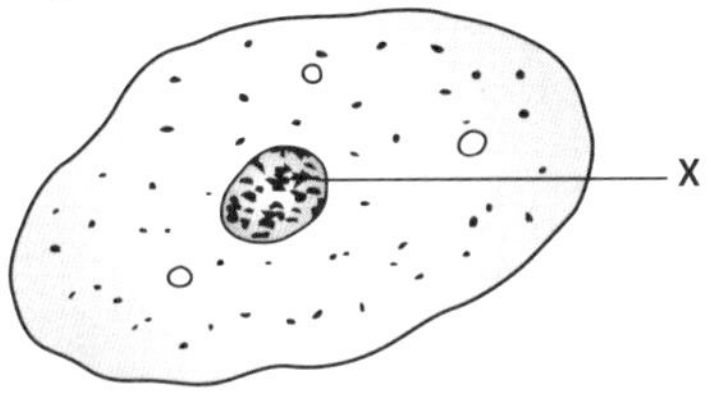

a vacuole
b nucleus
c chloroplast
d cytoplasm

3 This diagram shows a cross-section through a leaf:

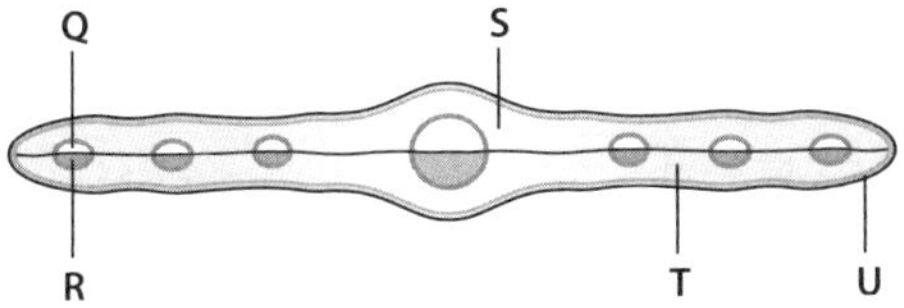

Identify the palisade mesophyll, phloem, and lower epidermis.

a palisade mesophyll = S; phloem = Q; lower epidermis = U

b palisade mesophyll = S; phloem = R; lower epidermis = U

c palisade mesophyll = T; phloem = E; lower epidermis = S

d palisade mesophyll = T; phloem = Q; lower epidermis = U

4 Identify the order in which body systems are built.

a cells → tissue → organs → body systems

b cells → organs → tissue → body systems

c organs → cells → tissue → body systems

d organs → tissue → cells → body systems

5 Name the process of removing waste from the human body.

a digestion
b respiration
c excretion
d reproduction

6 Which of the following does **not** contain cells?

a sand
b leaves
c skin
d heart

7 Complete this sentence: A bone is an example of…

a …a cell
b …tissue
c …an organ
d …body system

8 Complete this sentence: Red blood cells…

a …have a nucleus

b …live for a short period of time

c …carry carbon dioxide to the cells of the body

d …can change their shape and fight against infection in the body

9 What type of structure is the heart?
a cell
b organ
c tissue
d body system

10 What substance gives plants their green colour?
a haemoglobin
b chlorophyll
c mitochondria
d cytoplasm

11 What is the name of the pigment found in red blood cells?
a haemoglobin
b chlorophyll
c mitochondria
d cytoplasm

12 What are red blood cells also known as?
a phagocytes
b haemoglobin
c leukocytes
d erythrocytes

13 Name the muscles responsible for the movement of the body.
a cardiac
b skeletal
c smooth
d rough

14 Which of the following is **not** found in an animal cell?
a cell membrane
b chloroplast
c vacuole
d cytoplasm

Use the diagram below to answer questions 15 and 16.

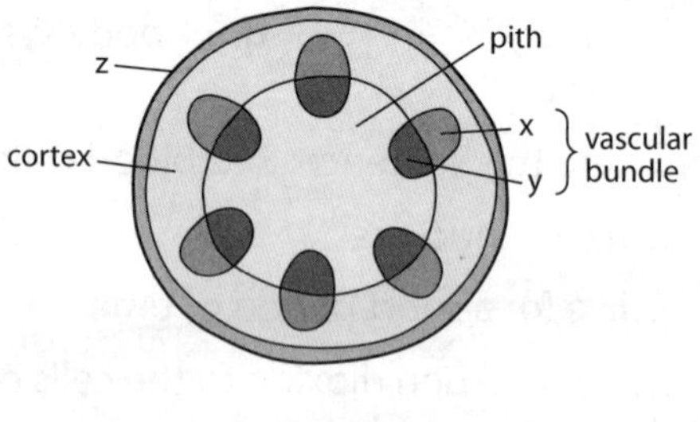

15 What does this image represent?
a cross-section of a leaf
b cross-section of a dicot root
c cross-section of a dicot stem
d cross-section of an onion

16 Which structures are represented by the letters X and Y?
a X = xylem; Y = phloem
b X = phloem; Y = xylem
c X= xylem; Y = cambium
d X = phloem; Y = epidermis

17 Which of these sets of organs make up the respiratory system?
a tongue, lungs, heart, and ribs
b trachea, bronchi, lungs, and diaphragm
c heart, lungs, trachea, and ribs
d tongue, trachea, heart, and diaphragm

18 This diagram shows one of the largest specialised mammalian cells. Which one?

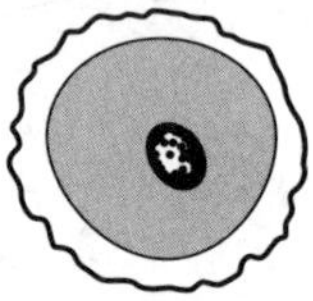

a sperm cell
b root hair cell
c muscle cell
d ovum

19 Name the human male reproductive cell.
a tadpole
b ovum
c egg
d sperm

20 Which of the following statements about cells or body systems is **not** correct?
a a group of similar cells carrying out the same function is known as a tissue
b the circulatory system transports food and nutrients around the body
c all cells have a cell wall, cell membrane, and a nucleus
d the digestive system begins at the mouth and ends at the anus

21 Which of the following lists only contains structures from the human reproductive system?

- **a** diaphragm; kidneys; bladder; ovaries
- **b** ovaries; testes; bladder; spinal cord
- **c** ovaries; penis; testes; fallopian tubes
- **d** kidney; urethra; sperm tube; vagina

22 When someone has the 'flu, which is most likely to occur?

- **a** red blood cells die
- **b** white blood cells multiply
- **c** red blood cells multiply
- **d** white blood cells consume red blood cells

23 Name the tubes through which water is transported up plants.

- **a** phloem
- **b** veins
- **c** pipes
- **d** xylem

24 Select the correct match between the organelle and its function.

- **a** mitochondria – photosynthesis
- **b** nucleus – respiration
- **c** chloroplast – manufacture of proteins
- **d** vacuole – storage

25 Helen wants to observe onion cells. What instrument should she use?

- **a** binoculars
- **b** magnifying lens
- **c** microscope
- **d** flashlight

Use the diagram below to answer questions 26, 27 and 28.

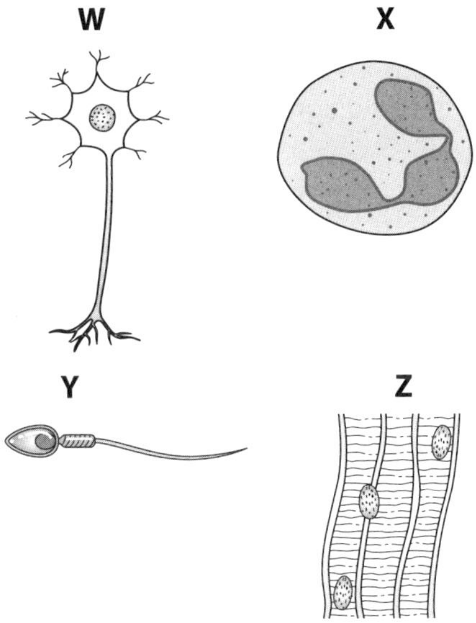

26 Which cell represents a white blood cell?

a W **b** X **c** Y **d** Z

27 Which cell has the function of transporting quick messages around the body?

a W **b** X **c** Y **d** Z

28 Identify the structure which has cells that can contract.

a W **b** X **c** Y **d** Z

29 Which cell structure is the site where energy is produced during respiration?

- **a** mitochondria
- **b** vacuole
- **c** chloroplast
- **d** nucleus

30 What is the main function of the cell wall?

- **a** protects and supports the cell
- **b** makes protein
- **c** converts energy from sunlight into chemical energy
- **d** takes in oxygen gas

Structured questions

Write your answers in the spaces provided.

1 Look at this diagram of a cell, then answer the questions that follow.

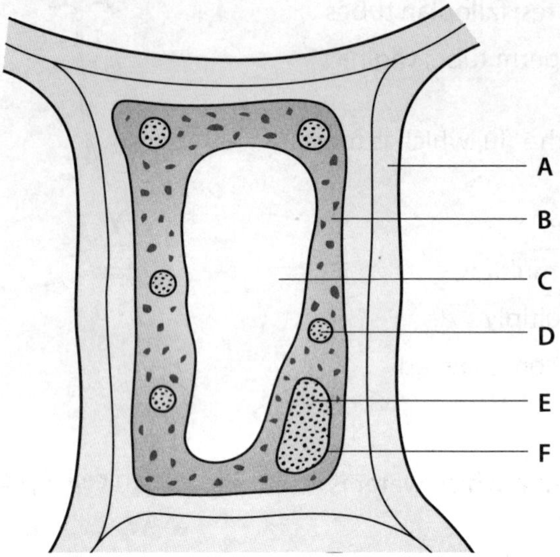

a What type of cell is shown in the diagram? ____________________

b Label structures A–F.

A ____________________ B ____________________

C ____________________ D ____________________

E ____________________ F ____________________

c State the function of structure F in the cell.

____

____

d I Name the liquid found in structure C. ____________________

II What substances are dissolved in the liquid found in C?

____

e What is the name of the green pigment found in structure D? ____________________

f Label this diagram to show the similarities and differences between a plant cell and an animal cell.

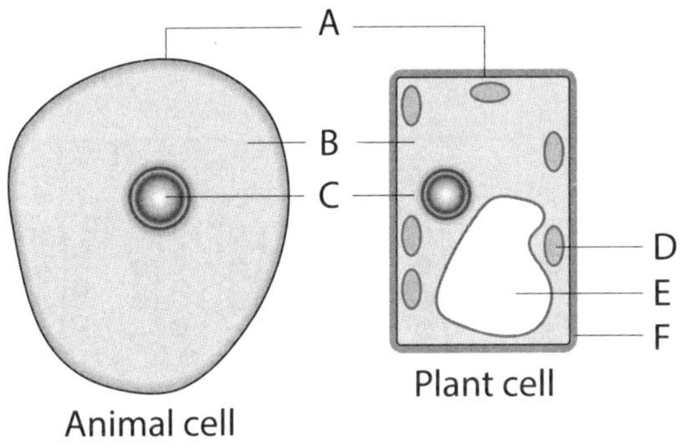

Found in animal and plant cells

A ________________

B ________________

C ________________

Found in plant cells only

D ________________

E ________________

F ________________

2 a Approximately how long do red blood cells live for? ________________

b Give **one** reason why red blood cells only live for a short period.

____

c Suzanne is a seemingly healthy teenager. However, she has about 5% more white blood cells in her blood than would be expected. Her doctor is showing concern. Explain why her doctor might be concerned.

____

____

3 Students observed two animal cells. They counted 500 mitochondria in cell A and 1,500 mitochondria in cell B.

a What is the function of the mitochondria in a cell?

____

b Give **one** reason why cell B may have more mitochondria than cell A.

____

____

c State, with reasons, which of the cells was a sperm cell and which was an ovum.

Cell A: ________________

Reason: ________________________________

____

Cell B: ________________

Reason: ________________________________

____

d Where in the sperm cell would you find mitochondria?

____

4 Look at this diagram of a cross-section though a leaf.

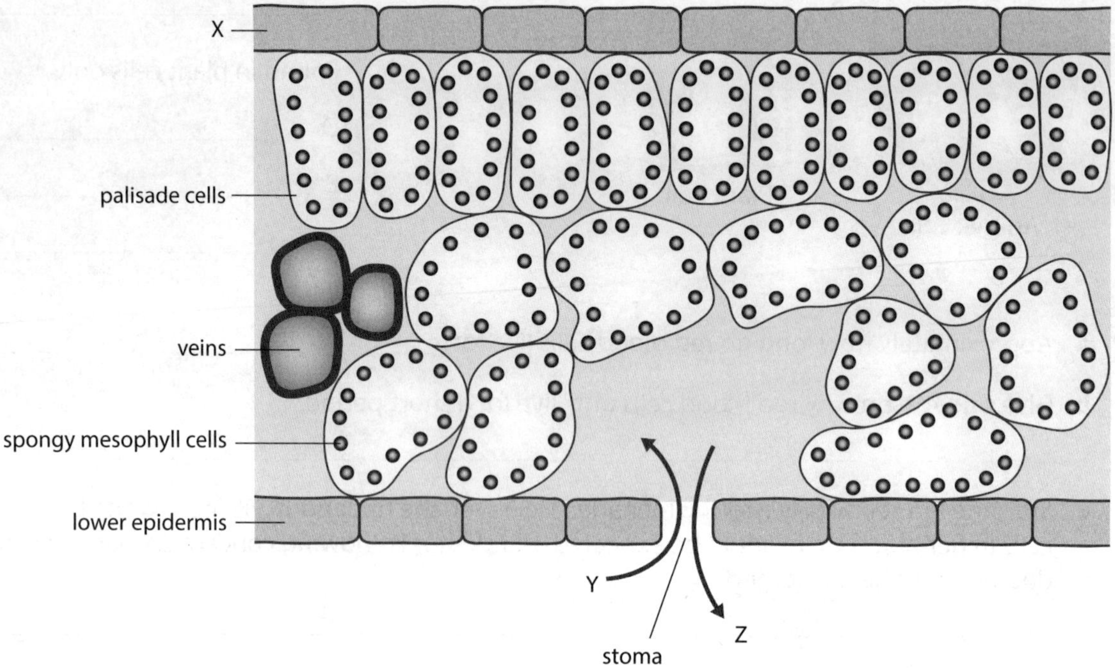

a Label structure X.

X ____________________

b Explain how the palisade layer has been adapted for photosynthesis.

____

____

____

c Explain why the cells in the spongy layer are loosely packed.

____

____

____

d Y and Z are gases that are found in air. Identify Y and Z.

Y ____________________

Z ____________________

5 Look at this diagram of an organ system found in the human body.

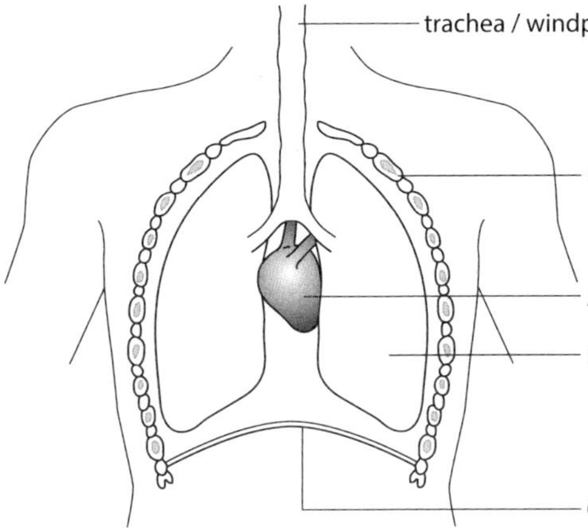

a What type of body system is represented by the diagram?

____

b Label structures A–C.

A ______________ B ______________ C ______________

6 a Complete the table by stating the function of the different body systems.

Organ system	Function
Circulatory	
Respiratory	
Digestive	
Nervous	

b Name the body system to which each these organ groups belongs.

I brain, spinal cord ______________

II stomach, intestines, pancreas ______________

III fallopian tube, uterus, ovary ______________

IV heart, blood vessels ______________

V penis, testes ______________

Investigative comprehension

Read the comprehension passage and answer the questions that follow.

Observing cheek cells

During a science lesson, Joan observed her own cheek cells using a microscope.

Joan collected the cells by gently rubbing the side of a toothpick against the inside of her cheek and spread the sample over the centre of a clean microscope slide. She then added methylene blue to stain the cells, and carefully covered it with a cover slip, making sure to start at an angle to avoid bubbles forming. She placed the prepared slide on the microscope stage.

Joan saw lots of cheek cells through the microscope. They each had an irregular shape, surrounded by a thin membrane. Inside each cell, there was a dark, oval nucleus within the cytoplasm, which was stained light blue. Joan also observed tiny blue-stained rods and spheres. She carried out some research and discovered that they were bacteria.

Finally, Joan drew a single cheek cell and labelled it.

1 Write an aim for the experiment.

____

2 Label structures A–E on this diagram of a microscope.

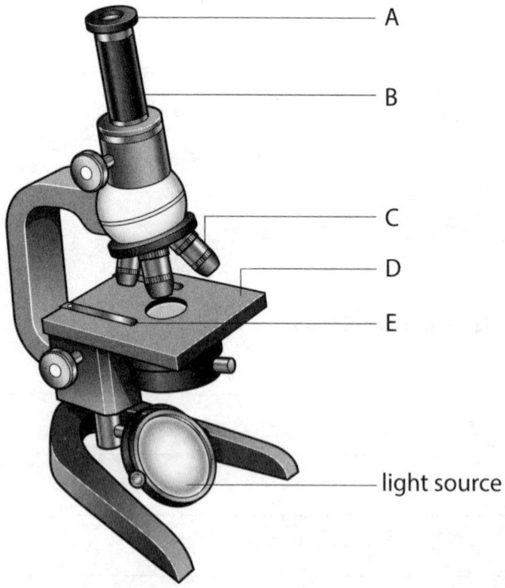

A ______________________

B ______________________

C ______________________

D ______________________

E ______________________

3 Explain how Joan could have changed the magnification of her sample.

____

____

4 What is the term used for a sample which has been spread over a microscope slide?

____

5 Why was the cheek sample stained?

____

6 Describe how to put a cover slip on a slide to avoid bubbles forming over a sample.

____

7 Label structures X, Y and Z on this diagram of a cheek cell.

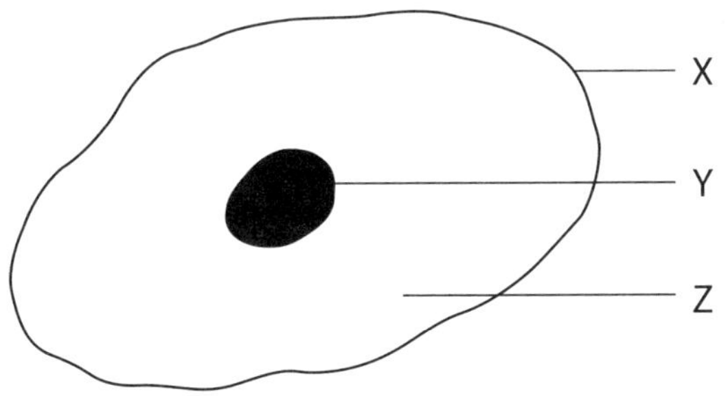

X _______________

Y _______________

Z _______________

8 **a** Where is DNA located in the cell? _______________

b State the purpose of DNA in the cell.

____

9 Carry out some research to find out more about bacteria.

a What is bacteria?

____

b What is the most common bacteria found in the human mouth?

____

c How many different species of bacteria are found in the human mouth?

____

d Explain the importance of having bacteria in the mouth.

____

____

e Describe some of the negative effects of harmful bacteria in the mouth.

____

____

True or false?

State whether each statement is true or false.

1 A unicellular organism is made up of many cells. ____________

2 A human male reproductive cell is called the sperm. ____________

3 Mitochondria produces the energy needed by cells. ____________

4 Bone is an example of a tissue. ____________

5 The nucleus controls what enters or leaves the cell. ____________

6 The cell wall and mitochondria are structures found only in plant cells. ____________

7 All living things are made up of tiny units called cells. ____________

8 Cells with similar functions group together to form tissue. ____________

9 Cardiac muscle makes up bones. ____________

10 Nerve cells carry messages around the body as electrical impulses. ____________

What am I?

Write the name of who or what the statement refers to.

1 A jelly-like mass in which all cell structures are found. ____________

2 The place where energy is released in cells. ____________

3 The pigment that make plants green. ____________

4 A simple structure that stores the cell sap. ____________

5 A cell without a cell wall. ____________

6 Lives for about 120 days and carries oxygen to the cells in the body. ____________

7 Hair-like projections from the roots of plants that are used to collect water and dissolved minerals from the soil. ____________

8 The ability of living things to respond to their environment. ____________

Matching

Draw lines to connect the diagram of each specialised cell with its correct name.

Diagram	Name
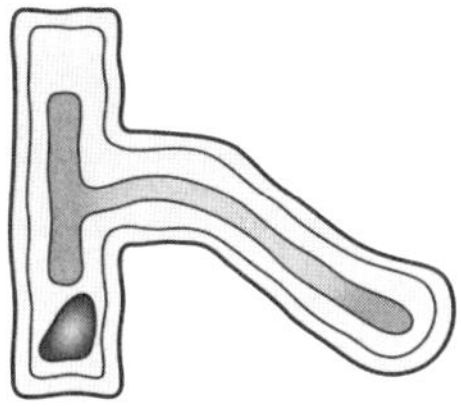	white blood cell
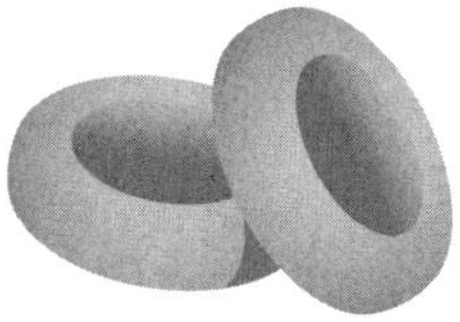	nerve cell
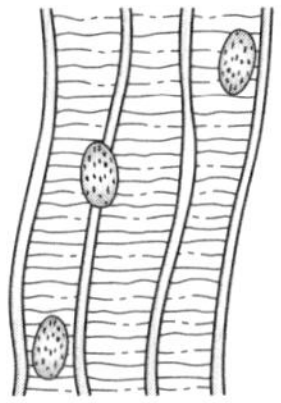	sperm cell
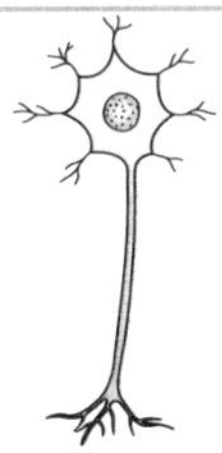	red blood cell
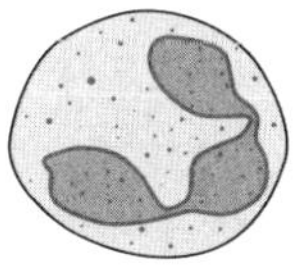	root hair cell
	skeletal muscle cell

Fill in the blanks

Complete the passage using the words below. Some words can be used once, more than once or not at all.

stimuli unicellular cells specialised animals chloroplast protection energy chlorophyll chemicals multicellular nervous photosynthesis heat

All living things are made up of ______________________.

Some organisms exist as a single cell and are called ______________________ organisms.

However, all animals and plants are ______________________ organisms. In other words, they are made up of many ______________________ grouped together. In multicellular organisms, different types of cells carry out ______________________ functions.

Living organisms have the ability to sense changes or ______________________ in their environment; they respond to keep themselves safe. Stimuli that we respond to include light, touch, sound, and ______________________. The ______________________ system plays an important role in helping us to respond quickly to stimuli.

Animal cells have no cell wall and they do not have any ______________________. Plant cells have a cell wall that provides support and ______________________. In a plant cell, the chloroplast contains a pigment called ______________________. It absorbs the energy from sunlight during ______________________ to make food for the plant.

Developing a scientific mind

1 Create a booklet on the topic *Characteristics of living organisms*. Include diagrams or photographs to illustrate characteristics where possible.

- Before starting, write a list of the things you will need to make your booklet.
- Once you have completed your booklet, present your project to your teacher.

2 Make a model of a plant or animal cell.

- Select suitable materials to represent the different organelles.
- Label all the structures you have placed in your cell.

3 Compose a song or rap about body systems. Remember to include all the following elements: cells, tissues, organs, organ systems and organisms.

Crossword

Across

1. Controls everything that happens in the cell.
2. Contains a liquid called cell sap.
6. They are produced by some types of white blood cells.
9. Jelly-like mass in which all cell structures are found.
10. The building block of all living things.
11. The name for red blood cells.
12. The female human gamete.
13. The green pigment in plants.
14. Group of similar cells working together.

Down

1. These cells are specialised to carry messages very quickly around the body.
3. Groups of tissue working together.
4. Tube that transports food from the leaves to the rest of the plant.
5. An instrument used to magnify cells.
7. The male human gamete.
8. Tube that transports water up to the leaves in plants.

UNIT 4 Energy

Multiple choice questions

Circle the letter that *best* corresponds to the answer of your choice.

1 Identify the statement which best describes *kinetic energy*.

- **a** energy stored in the nucleus of an atom
- **b** chemical energy stored in substances
- **c** energy in motion
- **d** energy stored by an object because of its position

2 Select the energy transfer that occurs in a lit match.

- **a** chemical energy $\rightarrow$ light
- **b** chemical energy $\rightarrow$ light + heat
- **c** chemical energy $\rightarrow$ heat
- **d** kinetic energy $\rightarrow$ light + heat

3 Name the type of energy stored in food.

- **a** kinetic energy
- **b** chemical energy
- **c** potential energy
- **d** solar energy

4 Which of the following is **not** a renewable source of energy?

- **a** geothermal
- **b** wind
- **c** solar
- **d** natural gas

5 Name the energy produced by moving electrons.

- **a** chemical
- **b** electrical
- **c** solar
- **d** sound

6 Identify the energy source that can be made from the waste of animals.

- **a** biogas
- **b** coal
- **c** wood
- **d** fertiliser

7 What form of energy is released from the Sun?

- **a** electrical
- **b** light and heat
- **c** chemical
- **d** sound

8 What is the important *function* of chlorophyll in (green) plants?

- **a** to make plants green
- **b** to aid in photosynthesis
- **c** to aid in respiration
- **d** to keep plants warm

9 A student placed a drop of iodine on a piece of bread. What colour did the bread turn?

- **a** brown
- **b** green
- **c** red
- **d** blue-black

10 Which of the following alternative energy sources is not normally considered as renewable?

- **a** geothermal
- **b** nuclear
- **c** hydroelectric
- **d** wind

11 What is the energy source from which all the energy we use originates?

a plants **b** electricity
c wind turbines **d** the Sun

12 Identify the condition which is **not** caused by overexposure to the Sun's rays.

a skin cancer **b** cataracts
c diabetes **d** sunstroke

13 Which of the following is **not** a fossil fuel?

a coal **b** natural gas
c crude oil **d** wood

14 What is the source of solar energy?

a solar panels **b** solar cells
c the Sun **d** batteries

15 Fuels, before being burnt, store what form of energy?

a heat **b** light
c chemical **d** potential

16 Select another name for crude oil.

a natural gas
b fossil fuels
c refined petroleum
d hydrocarbons

17 Name the gas released during the burning of fuels.

a hydrogen **b** oxygen
c carbon dioxide **d** nitrogen

18 What is the International System (SI) unit for energy?

a newton **b** metre
c kilogram **d** joule

19 A machine used 20 J of energy to make a bicycle start. However, 6 J of energy was wasted as heat. What is the percentage efficiency of the machine?

a 30% **b** 75%
c 70% **d** 60%

20 Four jars are filled with equal volumes of hot water. Jar W has three layers of insulation, Jar X has two layers of insulation, Jar Y has one layer of insulation, and Jar Z has no insulation. In which jar would the temperature of the water decrease most quickly?

a W **b** X **c** Y **d** Z

21 What gas is required for combustion (burning)?

a carbon dioxide **b** oxygen
c carbon monoxide **d** hydrogen

22 Which of the following substances is *least* likely to burn?

a glass **b** wood
c paper **d** cotton fibre

23 Which of the following is a *disadvantage* of wind energy?

a there are no fuel costs
b it is not very reliable
c it produces a lot of energy without polluting the environment
d it is a renewable energy source

24 Solar cells convert light energy directly into what?

a hot water **b** fire
c steam **d** electrical energy

25 Which example is a *non-renewable* energy source?

- **a** wind
- **b** solar
- **c** crude oil
- **d** geothermal

26 How is geothermal energy obtained?

- **a** by solar cells capturing sunlight
- **b** by heat from the Earth heating water to produce steam
- **c** by pumping it from under to above the Earth's surface
- **d** by mining from under the Earth's surface and burning to release the energy

27 Which of the following can **not** be made from petroleum?

- **a** iron
- **b** wax
- **c** gasoline
- **d** plastic bags

28 What temperature can a solar furnace reach?

- **a** 3,000 °C
- **b** 100 °C
- **c** 78 °C
- **d** 500 °C

29 Select an example of a natural gas.

- **a** kerosene
- **b** diesel
- **c** gasoline
- **d** methane

30 Complete this sentence: Burning is an example of a…

- **a** …chemical change
- **b** …physical change
- **c** …reversible reaction
- **d** …sublimation

Structured questions

Write your answers in the spaces provided.

1 a I State the difference between *renewable* and *non-renewable* sources of energy.

II Name two renewable sources of energy.

III Name two non-renewable sources of energy.

b I State the difference between a *renewable* and *alternative* energy source?

II Briefly explain the importance of alternative energy solutions to Jamaica.

c Briefly explain how the energy from the wind can be converted to electricity.

2 This diagram shows the set-up of a homemade solar panel.

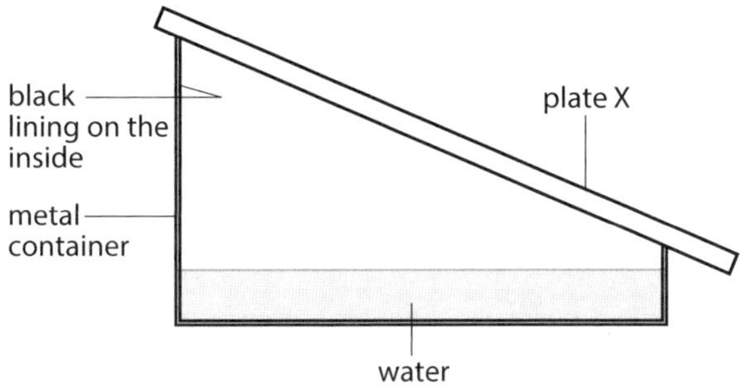

a Explain why a metal dish is used as the framework of the solar panel.

____

____

b What is the function of the black lining?

____

c Explain what happens to the water vapour after hitting plate X.

____

____

d Name **one** suitable material to make plate X. ______________________________

3 a What is a *fuel* and what type of energy does it contain?

____

____

b Name **three** fuels used in the home.

____

____

c Explain what crude oil is, including how it is extracted from beneath the Earth's surface.

____

____

____

4 a What does it mean to *conserve energy*?

____

____

____

b Give **two** reasons why we should conserve energy.

____

____

c Name **two** appliances used in the home that use a lot of energy.

____

____

d State **four** ways in which you can conserve energy in the home.

____

____

____

____

e Why does a refrigerator have insulation in its outer casing?

____

____

f Your neighbour noticed that he has been using more electricity since installing his electric water heater. He needs to reduce his electric bill. Suggest to your neighbour a cheaper and more affordable method of getting hot water for his home.

____

____

____

Investigative comprehension

Read the comprehension passage and answer the questions that follow.

Toy cars and kinetic energy

Mr. Morris asked his students to determine the kinetic energy of a battery-operated toy car. There were no instruments in the laboratory to measure the kinetic energy of the toy car directly. So, the students had to research ways to calculate it.

The students discovered that they needed to know the mass of the car and the average speed of the car when it was moving. They also discovered that the unit of energy is Joules, J.

Using this information, the students developed their investigation. First, they measured the mass of the toy car, using an electronic balance. Then, they calculated its speed. They measured the time it took for the car to travel a known distance, and used the equation:

$$\text{speed} = \frac{\text{distance}}{\text{time}}$$

Finally, they calculated the car's kinetic energy when moving. They used the equation:

$$\text{kinetic energy} = \frac{1}{2} \times \text{mass} \times \text{speed}^2$$

The students then noted some other observations from the investigation. They noticed that the car became warm after racing, and that it made a noise as it moved. The students asked Mr. Morris about their observations. He reminded them about the Law of Conservation of Energy.

1 Write a hypothesis for the investigation.

____

____

2 State the Law of Conservation of Energy.

____

3 Fill in the flow diagram to show the conversion of energy in the battery-operated toy car.

______________ → ______________ + ______________ + ______________

4 These diagrams show the measurements that the students made. Read the instruments and complete the table.

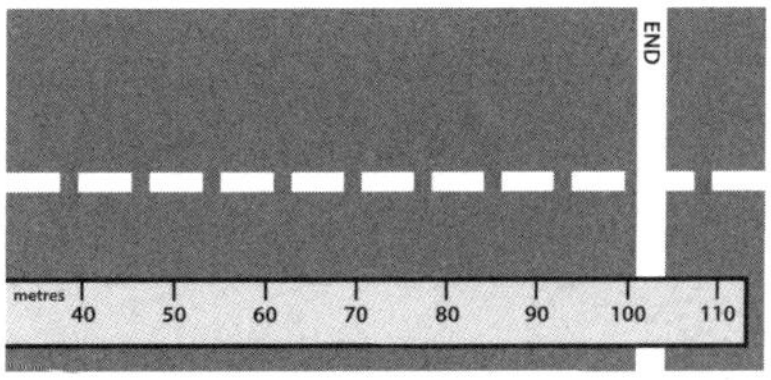

Quantity measured	value	units
Distance		
Time		
Mass		

5 Use the first equation in the passage to calculate the speed of the car.

$$\text{speed} = \frac{\text{distance}}{\text{time}} = \frac{\_\_\_\_\_\_}{\_\_\_\_\_\_} = \_\_\_\_\_\_ \text{ m/s}$$

6 Use the second equation in the passage to calculate the kinetic energy (KE) of the moving car.

$$\text{KE} = \frac{1}{2} \times \text{mass} \times \text{speed}^2$$

a write in the values for mass and speed $\text{KE} = \frac{1}{2} \times \_\_\_\_\_ \times \_\_\_\_\_^2$

b calculate the value for speed^2 $\text{KE} = \frac{1}{2} \times \_\_\_\_\_ \times \_\_\_\_\_$

c calculate the value for mass × speed^2 $\text{KE} = \frac{1}{2} \times \_\_\_\_\_$

d calculate the kinetic energy $\text{KE} = \_\_\_\_\_ \text{ J}$

7 a What forms of energy were considered *wasted* in this investigation?

____

____

b Why were these forms of energy considered *wasted*?

____

____

c Mr. Morris told the class that the input energy, from the battery, was 100 J.

The useful output energy was the KE, as calculated in question 6.

Calculate the amount of wasted output energy.

wasted output energy = input energy – useful output energy

wasted output energy = _____ J – _____ J = _____ J

True or false?

State whether each statement is true or false.

1 Potential energy is energy in motion. ____________

2 Electricity is produced by moving electrons. ____________

3 Energy can be created but not destroyed. ____________

4 Humans need energy to eat, move, and to stay alive. ____________

5 Solar cells convert sunlight into electric energy. ____________

6 Non-renewable energy will never run out. ____________

7 Oil is a non-renewable source of energy. ____________

8 Crude oil is a liquid mixture of hydrocarbons. ____________

9 Anthracite is the lowest grade of coal. ____________

10 Carbon dioxide is essential for burning. ____________

What am I?

Write the name of who or what the statement refers to.

1 Stored energy in food. ____________

2 Created from the bodies of tiny sea animals subjected to heat and pressure over millions of years. ____________

3 Turns in the wind to spin a generator and produce electricity. ____________

4 Premature wrinkling due to overexposure to the Sun. ____________

5 Energy produced from the gravitational force of falling water. ____________

6 Often wasted during energy conversions. ____________

7 Unit of energy. ____________

8 Materials that reduce the transfer of heat. ____________

Matching

Draw lines to connect the type of energy with its description.

Type of energy
potential
kinetic
nuclear
chemical
sound
electrical
solar
light

Description
energy stored in the nucleus of atoms
energy stored in substances such as food
energy stored by an object because of its position
energy from the Sun
energy in moving objects
energy that enables us to see
energy possessed by moving electrons
energy produced when things vibrate

Fill in the blanks

Complete the passage using the words below. Some words can be used once, more than once or not at all.

distillation fossil wood crude heat drilling plants coal hydrocarbons pressure propane millions oil

Fuels are substances that release ______________________ energy when they are burned. Naturally occurring fuels are called ______________________ fuels. Examples include ______________________, crude oil, and natural gas. They are formed from remains of plants and animals that have been subjected to a lot of heat and ______________________ under the Earth over a period of ______________________ of years.

Crude oil is a liquid mixture of ______________________. These are separated into useful products, such as fuels, using a process called fractional ______________________.

Crude oil is extracted from the Earth's crust by ______________________ wells and then using an oil rig to pump the oil to the surface. Crude oil can be separated and processed into useful substances such as diesel oil, wax and asphalt, and gases such as ______________________.

Developing a scientific mind

1 Design and create a card- or board-game about energy transfer.

- Give the game a name.
- Write down how to play the game, and the rules of the game.
- Make a list of all the things you will need to create your energy conversion game.
- Play your game with some of your classmates.

2 Working in a group of three or four, write a skit or short play on the importance of conserving energy in the home. It should be about five minutes long. It should only consist of three or four characters. It should be accurate, realistic, captivating and clear.

Crossword puzzle

Across

2. Energy stored in the nucleus of atoms.
4. A substance that releases heat energy when burned.
6. Sources of which are not easily depleted and do not pollute the environment.
7. Energy in motion.
11. Substances found in crude oil.
13. Using moving water to generate electricity.
14. Energy produced from moving electrons.
16. Chemical energy is stored in this part of a candle.
17. Ability to do work.

Down

1. Energy stored in fuels.
3. Ensure not to waste energy.
5. There is 50–75% of this gas in the typical composition of biogas.
8. The process by which coal is formed.
9. Energy from the Sun.
10. Another term used for crude oil.
12. The original energy source.
13. An effect of over exposure to the Sun.
15. An example of a fossil fuel.

UNIT 5 Plant reproduction

Multiple choice questions

Circle the letter that *best* corresponds to the answer of your choice.

1 Where are the male and female reproductive structures of a plant located?

a in its seeds **b** in its flowers
c in its leaves **d** in its fruit

2 Identify the statement that best describes a function of the veins in a plant's leaves.

a decorate the leaves
b transport energy to the cells in the leaves
c help support the structure of the leaves
d help to keep the plant cool

3 Which of these storage organs is a *rhizome*?

a carrot **b** ginger
c onion **d** potato

4 Complete this sentence: Banana trees can reproduce asexually by producing…

a …seeds **b** …suckers
c …bulbs **d** …flowers

5 What is sweet potato an example of?

a root tuber **b** rhizome
c bulb **d** taproot

6 In what form do plants store the food they make?

a cellulose **b** carbohydrates
c sugar **d** starch

7 Martina placed a drop of iodine on a food substance. The colour changed to blue-black. What does this indicate the presence of?

a glucose **b** sucrose
c starch **d** cellulose

8 What is the male reproductive organ of a flower called?

a stamen **b** style
c stigma **d** filament

9 Name the swollen tip of the stem on which the flower is held.

a radicle **b** receptacle
c ovary **d** radial

10 Which structures make up the *female* reproductive organ of the flower?

a anther; filament
b stigma; anther; filament
c stigma; style; filament
d stigma; style; ovary

11 Which structures make up the *male* reproductive organ of the flower?

a anther; filament
b stigma; anther; filament
c stigma; style; filament
d stigma; style; ovary

12 Pollen grains are found in which part of the flower?

a ovary
b anther
c stigma
d filament

13 What transfer takes place during the process of *pollination*?

a anther to ovary
b pollen grain to stigma
c pollen grain to ovary
d pollen grain to style

14 What is the chemical equation of photosynthesis?

a glucose + energy → carbon dioxide + water
b glucose + carbon dioxide → water + oxygen + energy
c glucose + water → oxygen + carbon dioxide + energy
d carbon dioxide + water → glucose + oxygen

15 Which statement best defines the process of *germination*?

a a seed grows into a new plant
b pollen transfers to the stigma
c a plant dies
d a new plant grows from part of the structure of the plant

16 Name the release of water vapour through the stomata of a plant's leaves.

a transpiration
b respiration
c transportation
d photosynthesis

17 Where does photosynthesis take place?

a leaf
b root
c stem
d flower

18 Identify the name given to a flower that contains *both* male and female reproductive structures.

a perfect flower
b imperfect flower
c incomplete flower
d complete flower

19 Identify the statement that best outlines the role of plants in the environment.

a plants beautify the environment
b plants provide habits for many organisms
c plants produce oxygen used by humans and animals in respiration
d all of the above

Use the diagram below to answer questions 20 and 21.

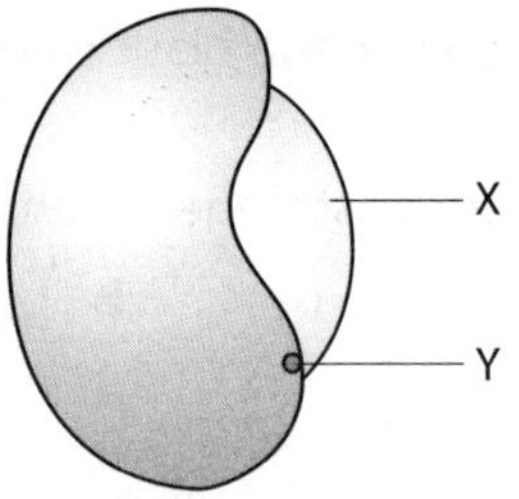

20 What is the structure labelled X in the diagram above?

a hilum
b plumule
c micropyle
d testa

21 What is the function of structure Y in the diagram above?

a allows the seed to breathe
b allows carbon dioxide to enter the seed
c allows water to enter the seed during germination
d allows water to exit the seed during germination

22 Complete this sentence: A seed produced by a dicotyledonous plant will...

a ...have a flat surface

b ...have narrow seed leaves

c ...have only one seed leaf

d ...have two seed leaves

23 Which of the following is **not** a necessary condition for germination?

a water **b** sunlight

c temperature **d** oxygen

24 What is the reproductive structure of flowering plants called?

a leaf **b** root

c stem **d** flower

25 Which part of the flower contains the ovule?

a stigma **b** ovary

c style **d** petal

26 What is the name of the leaf-like structure that protects a flower in the bud stage?

a petals **b** ovary

c sepals **d** petiole

27 What part of the flower becomes the fruit after fertilisation?

a seed **b** style

c stigma **d** ovary

28 Where are pollens stored in the flower?

a anther **b** style

c stigma **d** ovary

29 What is the protective coat of a seed called?

a micropyle **b** testa

c hilum **d** plumule

30 What part of the seed will grow into the shoot of the new plant?

a cotyledons **b** radicle

c hilum **d** plumule

Structured questions

Write your answers in the spaces provided.

1 This diagram shows the internal structures of two seeds, X and Y.

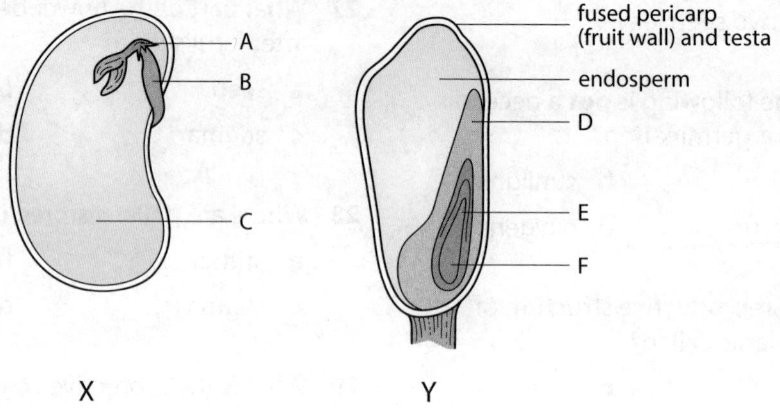

a Label structures A–F.

A ______ B ______ C ______

D ______ E ______ F ______

b What are the functions of structures C and D?

______

______

c Which structures will give rise to the roots of the new plant?

______

______

d Which seed comes from a monocotyledonous plant? Give **one** reason for your answer.

______

______

______

e What is *endosperm*?

______

f What does endosperm consist of?

______

______

2 This diagram shows the external structures of a flower.

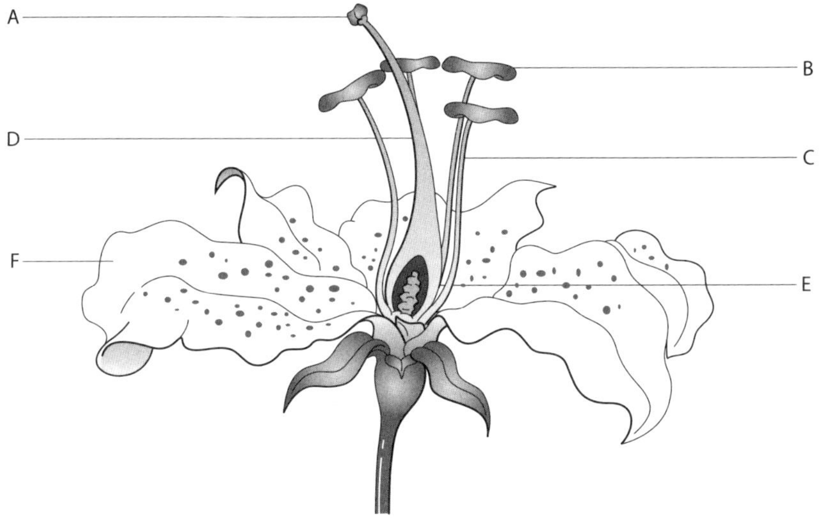

a Label structures A–F.

A ______________ B ______________ C ______________

D ______________ E ______________ F ______________

b Give **one** reason why F is brightly coloured.

____

c Give **one** reason why insects and humming birds visit this flower regularly.

____

d Name the male reproductive structure of the flower and list its structures.

____

____

____

e Name the female reproductive structure of the flower and list its structures.

____

____

____

f State **one** use of flowers, other than for decoration.

____

3 This question involves fieldwork. Select **five** different flowers from the environment around you, such as hibiscus, grass, and pride of Barbados. In the table on the following page, record the number of floral parts for each flower you select. State whether you think the flower is wind- or insect-pollinated, giving a reason for your choice.

Name of flower	Number of floral structures				Wind- or insect-pollinated?	Reason
	Petals	Sepals	Stamens	Pistils		

4 **a** Complete labels A–D on this diagram showing how fertilisation occurs in a flower.

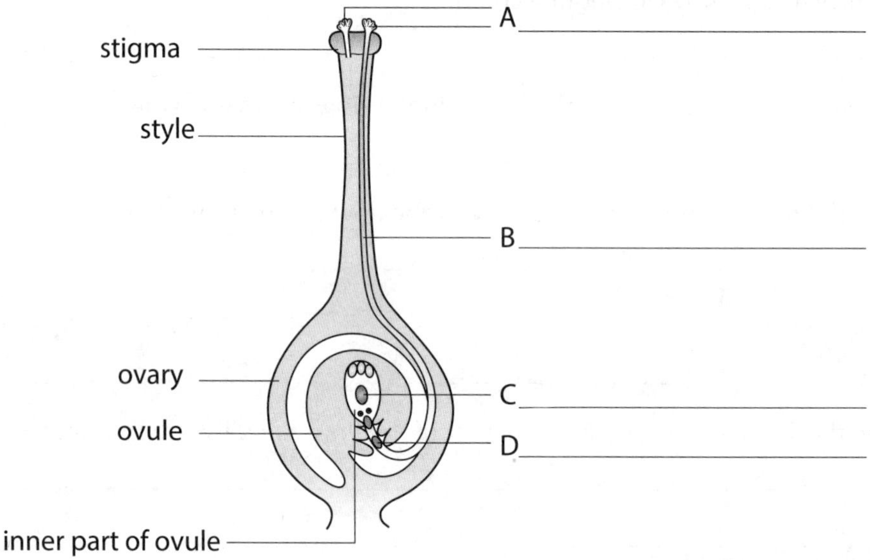

b What is the function of structure B?

c What happens to the ovule after it is fertilised?

d What part of the flower becomes the fruit after fertilisation?

Investigative comprehension

Read the comprehension passage and answer the questions that follow.

Observing how seeds grow

Christopher is a Grade 7 student at your school. He is very excited about science. One day, his science teacher explained the conditions necessary for seeds to grow into new plants. On his way home that evening, Christopher purchased some red peas at the market.

When Christopher got home, he decided to set up an experiment to observe how seeds grow. Before setting up the experiment, he removed the seed coat – also known as the testa – from one of the seeds. He noticed that the seed had two cotyledons which he separated; attached to one of the cotyledons was a young shoot and root. After observing the internal structure of the seed, he placed six red peas into a transparent jar containing cotton wool and left the jar open by his window. After two weeks, Christopher did not notice any changes in his red pea seeds.

Help Christopher by answering the following questions:

1 What is the name of the process of seeds developing into new plants?

____

2 What are the **three** conditions required for a seed to grow into a new plant?

____

____

3 Christopher's seeds didn't grow at his first attempt.

a Explain to Christopher *why* his red pea seeds did not grow.

____

____

b Advise Christopher how he can improve his experiment and get the red pea seeds to grow.

____

____

Following your advice, Christopher repeated the experiment. This time, the seeds began to germinate. First, he noticed that the seed became swollen and the testa eventually burst as the root came out. This was followed by the shoot, three days later.

He measured the growth of one plant over a period of 14 days and put his results in a table:

Number of days	**0**	**2**	**4**	**6**	**8**	**10**	**12**	**14**
Growth of seedling (cm)	0.0	0.0	1.0	3.0	7.1	13.9	20.0	22.5

4 Look at Christopher's table of results.

a State the units of measurement used for the length of the seedling.

Write your answer in words. ____________________

a What instrument would Christopher have used to measure the length of the seedling?

____

5 Plot a graph to show the growth of the seedling. Label the axes accurately, with *time (days)* on the *x*-axis and *growth (cm)* on the *y*-axis.

Give your graph a suitable title.

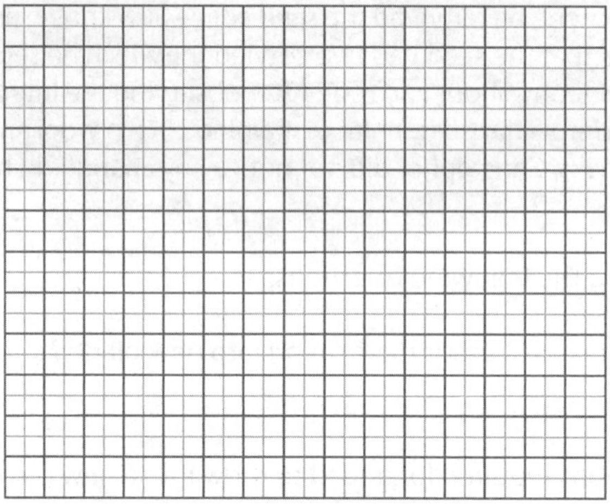

6 During what period did the seedling grow fastest?

____

7 Explain what might happen to the growth of the seedling after day 14.

____

____

8 Carry out some research to answer the following questions.

a Name the structures that make up the embryo of the seed.

____

b Create a plan for how you would look after the seedlings to ensure they develop into healthy plants.

____

____

____

____

True or false?

State whether each statement is true or false.

1 The anthers of wind-pollinated flowers are usually enclosed inside the flower. ______

2 Plants make starch during photosynthesis and store any excess as glucose. ______

3 The reproductive structures of flowering plants are found in the roots. ______

4 The stamen is the male reproductive structure of the flowering plant. ______

5 Sugar cane is a wind-pollinated plant. ______

6 The female reproductive structure consists of the anther and filament. ______

7 The plumule and radicle are the only structures that make up the embryo of a seed. ______

8 Fertilisation occurs before pollination in flowering plants. ______

9 The ovary becomes the fruit after fertilisation of flowering plants. ______

10 Carbon dioxide and glucose are the raw materials of photosynthesis. ______

What am I?

Write the name of who or what the statement refers to.

1 Contains the reproductive organ of flowering plants. ______

2 Plants use this for anchorage; it also helps supply water and minerals. ______

3 Reproduction without gametes. ______

4 A young plant. ______

5 The process by which pollen grains are transferred from the anther to the stigma of the flowers. ______

6 The process by which seeds grow into plants. ______

7 The part of the stamen which holds up the anther. ______

8 The process by which plants manufacture their own food. ______

Matching

Draw lines to connect the plant to the type of asexual reproduction method.

Plant	Reproduction method
 ginger	bulb
 banana	root tubers
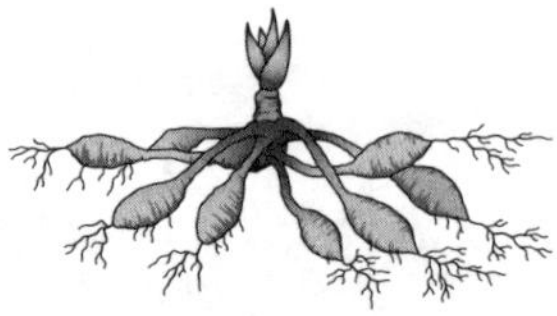 sweet potato	rhizome
 onion	suckers

Fill in the blanks

Complete the passage using the words below. Some words can be used once, more than once or not at all.

chlorophyll	water	soil	reproduction	photosynthesis	starch	roots	stem
blue-black	plant	energy	carbon	glucose	flowers	oxygen	organisms
flowering	sunlight	atmosphere					

Flowering plants consist of four main parts: flowers, leaves, stems, and ____________________.

The ____________________ provides support to the plant.

The ____________________ anchor the plants in the ground.

The flowers are important for ____________________.

The leaves contain a green pigment called ____________________ which traps light energy from the Sun for the process of ____________________.

During photosynthesis, ____________________ dioxide reacts with water to make ____________________.

Plants use some glucose during respiration and convert some into ____________________, which is stored as food. Photosynthesis also produces ____________________.

We can test for the presence of starch using iodine solution. Iodine turns ____________________ in the presence of starch.

Plants are very important. They play a major role in oxygen production and the removal of carbon dioxide from the ____________________. Plants are also used as foods and medicines for many ____________________, including humans.

Developing a scientific mind

1 Write an article for the local newspaper about the importance of plants in the environment. Include information about the importance of planting trees.

2 Create a three-dimensional model of a plant.

Label each of the main structures, stating their name and function. Make sure you include:

- leaf
- root
- stem
- fruit
- flowers

Cryptogram puzzle

Each letter in the phrase is linked to a specific number. Work out the letters linked with the other numbers and solve the phrase. Each phrase has a different letter-number combination. (HINT: Solve one letter at a time.)

1

A	B	C	D	E	F	G	H	I	J	K	L	M	N	O	P	Q	R	S	T	U	V	W	X	Y	Z
			2												3		25		19			14			

T _ _ (19 10 21) R _ _ _ P T _ _ _ _ (25 21 8 21 3 19 11 8 22 21) _ _ (6 18) T _ _ (19 10 21)

_ W _ _ _ _ _ (18 14 17 22 22 21 1) T _ P (19 6 3) _ _ (17 9) T _ _ (19 10 21) _ T _ _ (18 19 21 20)

_ _ (17 1) W _ _ _ _ (14 10 6 8 10) T _ _ (19 10 21) _ _ _ W _ R (9 22 17 14 21 25) _ _ (6 18) _ _ _ D (10 21 22 2)

2

A	B	C	D	E	F	G	H	I	J	K	L	M	N	O	P	Q	R	S	T	U	V	W	X	Y	Z
						26							2		21		4	3	18						

P _ _ _ _ N _ T _ _ N (21 11 10 10 17 2 19 18 17 11 2) _ S (17 3) T _ _ (18 16 7) T R _ N S _ _ R (18 4 19 2 3 13 7 19)

_ _ (11 13) P _ _ _ _ N (21 11 10 10 7 2) G R _ _ N S (26 4 19 17 2 3) _ R _ _ (13 4 11 23) T _ _ (18 16 7)

_ N T _ _ R (19 2 18 16 7 4) T _ (18 11) T _ _ (18 16 7) S T _ G _ _ (3 18 17 26 23 19) _ _ (11 13) T _ _ (18 16 7)

S _ _ _ (3 19 23 7) _ _ _ _ _ R (13 10 11 20 7 4) _ R (11 4) _ _ (11 13) _ (19) _ _ _ _ _ R _ N T (12 17 13 13 7 4 7 2 18)

_ _ _ _ _ R (13 10 11 20 7 4)

3

A	B	C	D	E	F	G	H	I	J	K	L	M	N	O	P	Q	R	S	T	U	V	W	X	Y	Z
		10		8		26		2			15														

_ _ I _ G _ (12 13 2 19 26 18) _ _ _ _ (12 13 17 12) _ _ _ I _ _ (17 18 18 2 18 12) _ I _ _ (5 2 12 13)

_ _ L L I _ _ _ I _ _ _ (4 11 15 15 2 19 17 12 2 11 19 18) _ _ C _ (18 22 10 13) _ _ (17 18) _ I _ _ (5 2 19 9)

_ _ (11 6) I _ _ E C _ _ (2 19 18 8 10 12 18) _ _ E (17 6 8) C _ L L E _ (10 17 15 15 8 9)

_ G E _ _ _ (17 26 8 19 12 18) _ _ (11 3) _ _ L L I _ _ _ I _ _ (4 11 15 15 2 19 17 12 2 11 19)

UNIT 6 Sexual maturity and reproduction in humans

Multiple choice questions

Circle the letter that *best* corresponds to the answer of your choice.

1 Select the female sex cell.

a sperm **b** ovum

c testicle **d** tadpole

2 Identify another name for the womb.

a oviduct **b** cervix

c vagina **d** uterus

3 What is the first menstrual cycle called?

a menstruation **b** menarche

c menses **d** menopause

4 What structures in the cells determine the characteristic of an individual?

a cellulose

b nucleus

c mitochondria

d genes in the chromosomes

5 There are six developmental stages in a human's lifetime. What is the *third* stage called?

a adolescence **b** childhood

c adulthood **d** old age

6 Which of the following parts of the body make up the trunk?

a arms and legs

b thorax and abdomen

c head and limbs

d abdomen and legs

7 Which statement best describes *puberty*?

a the time when sexual and physical characteristics develop in the body

b the stage when pimples start to show on boys and girls

c the stage just before birth when the child develops in the mother's womb

d the time between the age of two and 12 years when a child grows rapidly

8 Between which ages does the *baby stage* occur?

a birth to one year

b one to two years

c two to twelve years

d birth to six months

9 Complete this sentence: When a sperm fuses with an egg it is called…

a …a baby

b …a zygote

c …a foetus

d …an embryo

10 What is the *last* stage in the human life cycle?

a adolescence

b adulthood

c childhood

d old age

11 Complete this sentence: The chemicals released from glands in the body are called…

a …hormones **b** …ovum
c …sperm **d** …impulses

12 What is the *first* stage of the human cycle?

a foetus **b** old age
c adolescent **d** adulthood

13 Which of the following is **not** a structure of the head?

a eye **b** mouth
c nose **d** waist

14 Which stage of the human cycle starts with puberty?

a foetus **b** old age
c adolescent **d** adulthood

15 How does adolescence start?

a growth spurt
b deepening of the voice
c growing hair in the pubic region
d widening of the chest and hips

16 What is the male sex hormone called?

a gonadotropin
b testosterone
c oestrogen
d none of the above

17 What is the female sex hormone called?

a gonadotropin
b testosterone
c oestrogen
d none of the above

18 Identify the characteristic that does **not** occur with females during puberty.

a breasts grow
b menstruation begins
c broad shoulders develop
d hips broaden

19 Which of the following is **not** part of the male reproductive organ?

a penis **b** ovary
c testes **d** urethra

20 Identify the statement which best explains why the testes are located outside the body.

a sperms need a lot of air to be produced
b the production of sperm occurs best at 2 °C below normal body temperature
c sperms are produced once they get space to move around
d sperms are produced at atmospheric temperature

21 Which statement best describes the function of the *epididymis*?

a the place where sperm is produced
b gets rid of urine
c produces the fluids which make semen
d the place where sperm is stored after they are produced

22 What structure in the sperm contains genetic information?

a nucleus
b acrosome
c mitochondria
d tail

23 What is the function of the tail of the sperm?

a movement

b defence

c protection

d penetrating the ovum

24 Identify the statement that best describes the *oviduct*.

a pear-shaped organ

b tube about 10 cm long

c muscular canal that can stretch

d spherical glands located on either side of the uterus

25 The ovaries in the female reproductive system have a similar function to which structure in the male reproductive system?

a prostate gland **b** penis

c sperm **d** testes

26 What is another term for the fallopian tubes?

a ovaries **b** cervix

c uterus **d** oviduct

27 What is another term for the vagina?

a birth canal **b** womb

c menstruation **d** cervix

28 Complete this sentence: The release of a mature egg from the ovary is called…

a …menarche

b …menstruation

c …puberty

d …ovulation

29 At which stage can a woman no longer mature an egg?

a menopause **b** puberty

c menstruation **d** ovulation

30 Complete this sentence: Fertilisation in humans occurs when a sperm…

a …swims into the uterus

b …and an ovum fuse

c …enters the vagina

d …enters the fallopian tube

Structured questions

Write your answers in the spaces provided.

1 This is a diagram of the human male gamete.

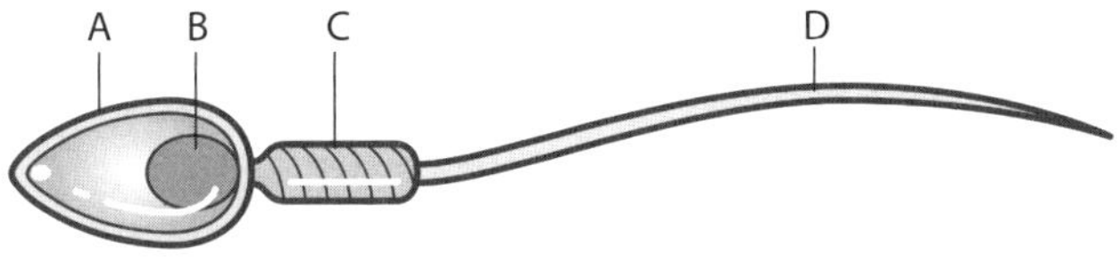

a What is the human male gamete called? ____________________

b Label structures A–D.

A ____________________ B ____________________

C ____________________ D ____________________

c Where is the genetic information located in the male gamete?

____

d What is the function of structure D?

____

e Explain why structure C consists of many mitochondria.

____

____

2 This is a diagram of the human male reproductive system.

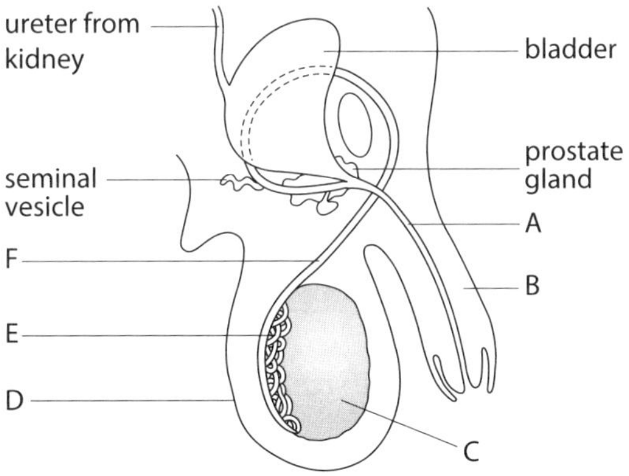

a Label structures A – F.

A ____________________ B ____________________ C ____________________

D ____________________ E ____________________ F ____________________

b Where are male sex cells made and then stored?

____

c State **two** functions of structure A.

____

____

3 This is a diagram of the human female reproductive system.

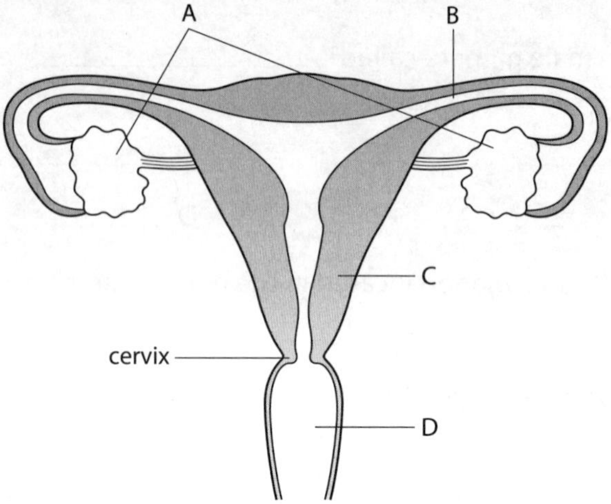

a Label structures A–D.

A ________________ B ________________

C ________________ D ________________

b State another name for structure C, and its function.

____

c In which structure are the sex cells located? ________________

d What is the function and approximate length of structure B?

____

____

e Which structure is also known as the *birth canal*? ________________

4 a Define the term *hygiene*.

____

____

____

____

b State **three** advantages of practicing good hygiene.

c Why would the Ministry of Health pay to advertise the importance of washing hands?

d Highlight the dangers of sharing your hair brush with other people at school.

Investigative comprehension

Read the comprehension passage and answer the questions that follow.

The menstrual cycle

The menstrual cycle starts when a girl reaches puberty. It is usually a 28-day cycle. Once a female starts her menstrual cycle, it is an indication that she is capable of reproducing.

Three things happen during the cycle.

1 Menstruation

Menstruation, or period (blood shed), occurs from day 1–4. It may last up to five days. Sanitary pads or tampons are used to absorb the flow. The soiled pads (or tampons) must be disposed of hygienically.

2 Follicular phase

The levels of the female sex hormone, oestrogen, increase and the soft-lining of the uterus thickens as it gets ready to receive an egg from the ovary. This process normal happens over 7–8 days.

3 Ovulation

Midway through the menstrual cycle, at day 14, the ovary releases a mature egg (ovum). If the released egg is not fertilised, the soft lining of the uterus continues to build up for another 14 days before breaking down and shedding through the vagina as menstruation.

The cycle, therefore, repeats from day one as blood flows from the uterus through the vagina.

Menstruation can start as early as nine years-old or as late as 15 years-old. An early or late start is nothing to worry about. The first menstrual cycle is called the menarche.

1 a What is the name given to the process in which blood is shed through the vagina?

____

b Outline the care or precautions that females should take during this process.

____

____

2 Explain what happens at about day 14 of the menstrual cycle.

____

____

3 Complete the menstrual cycle bracelet. The numbers in the beads represent the days in the menstrual cycle.

- Use a red crayon to colour the days when blood shed occurs.
- Use a green crayon to colour the stage where a mature egg is released from the ovary.
- Use a yellow crayon to colour the second stage of the menstrual cycle.
- Use a blue crayon to colour the final stage of the menstrual cycle.
- Complete the key by colouring the squares and writing the names of the stages beside them.

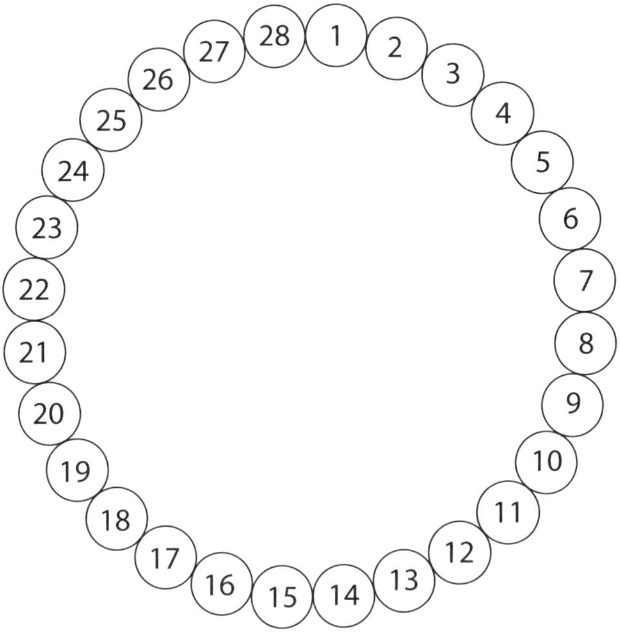

Key

☐ ______________

☐ ______________

☐ ______________

☐ ______________

4 Carry out some research to answer the following questions.

a Give the name of the hormone released from the pituitary gland during the second stage of the menstrual cycle.

____

b State **three** symptoms that a woman may experience while going through menopause

I ____

II ____

III ____

c State **one** thing that would end the menstrual cycle:

I temporarily

II permanently.

____

____

True or false?

State whether each statement is true or false.

1 A healthy male produces more than 100 million sperm daily. ____________

2 The penis allows for the passage of urine and sperm. ____________

3 Testosterone is the female sex hormone. ____________

4 The oviducts are the fallopian tubes. ____________

5 The vagina consists of a muscular wall. ____________

6 Ovaries and testes produce human sex cells. ____________

7 The testes are located inside the body on opposite sides of the prostate. ____________

8 The sperm duct transports sperm from the seminal vesicles to outside the body. ____________

9 The acrosome of the sperm contains enzymes to dissolve the membrane of the ovum. ____________

10 The cervix is a ring of muscles that closes the uterus from the vagina. ____________

What am I?

Write the name of who or what the statement refers to.

1 Also known as the birth canal. ____________

2 Occurs on about day 14 of each menstrual cycle. ____________

3 Houses the organ that produces the human male sex cells. ____________

4 A ring of muscles that closes the lower end of the uterus. ____________

5 The stage in the human cycle which starts with puberty. ____________

6 A chemical which is released into the blood from glands in the body. ____________

7 The hormone which starts the process of puberty. ____________

8 The structure where female gametes are stored until they are matured and released. ____________

Matching

Draw lines to connect the female reproductive structures with their equivalent male reproductive structure.

Female structures
vagina
ovary
oviduct
ovum
clitoris

Male structures
glans
sperm
penis
testis
sperm duct

Fill in the blanks

Complete the passage using the words below. Some words can be used once, more than once or not at all.

above warm sperm testes ovaries zygote oviducts million closer ova gametes
sexual inside uterus penis scrotum cervix below vagina

Humans reproduce by ______________ reproduction. This involves the fusion of male and female ______________ (sex cells).

The male gametes are called ______________. The female gametes are called ______________, or eggs.

Fertilisation occurs when a male and female gamete fuse. The fertilised egg is called a ______________.

The main structures of the male reproductive system are the penis, sperm duct, urethra, and ______________.

The testes are located outside of the body because sperm are best made at a temperature about 2°C ______________ normal body temperature. If the testes become very cold, scrotal sac muscles will pull the testes ______________ to the body to warm them up and to keep the sperm production at its optimum.

All the structures of the female reproductive system are located ______________ the female's body. The female reproductive system includes two glands, called ______________, which are connected on either side of the uterus (womb) by 10 cm long tubes called ______________.

The uterus joins to the ______________ by a ring of muscles at the neck of the womb called the ______________.

Developing a scientific mind

1 Create a jig saw puzzle of the male and female gametes.

- Draw and colour a labelled scientific drawing of the male and female gametes.
- Paste the image onto cardboard and allow to dry.
- Draw lines over the image to create at least ten interlocking pieces (you could do an internet search to find puzzle-piece images to trace).
- Use a suitable cutting instrument to cut out the interlocking pieces.

2 Create and perform a song about good personal hygiene. Once you have written your song, you should compare it with your classmates to see if you have made the same points.

Crossword puzzle

Across

4. A gum infection.
6. Another term used for uterus.
8. Fusion of a sperm and ovum.
9. The shedding of the lining of the uterus through the vagina.
11. The first menstrual cycle.
13. A fungal infection that leaves patches of hairless region on the scalp.

Down

1. Bad breath.
2. Birth canal.
3. The female sex cell.
5. A calcified yellow deposit around teeth.
7. The release of a mature egg from the ovary.
9. A period when a woman no longer has a menstrual cycle.
10. A structure in the nucleus of a cell that provides genetic information.
12. A ring of muscles at the base of the uterus.

UNIT 7 Sexually transmitted infections, and drugs

Multiple choice questions

Circle the letter that *best* corresponds to the answer of your choice.

1 Which of the following can be a pathogen?

- **a** bacteria
- **b** viruses
- **c** yeast
- **d** all of the above

2 Which of the following could be an impact of irresponsible sexual behaviour among young teens?

- **a** low self-esteem
- **b** embarrassment among their peers
- **c** emotional and psychological trauma
- **d** all of the above

3 Identify the option that indicates a responsible sexual behaviour for a young teen.

- **a** abstinence
- **b** unprotected sexual activity
- **c** having multiple sexual partners
- **d** publicly displaying sexual interactions

4 Which of the following sexually transmitted infections is **not** caused by bacteria?

- **a** AIDS
- **b** syphilis
- **c** gonorrhoea
- **d** chlamydia

5 Which sexually transmitted infection causes a yellow discharge from the genitals?

- **a** herpes
- **b** gonorrhoea
- **c** syphilis
- **d** AIDS

6 Which statement best describes a *drug*?

- **a** all chemical substances
- **b** illegal substances
- **c** chemical substances that change the way the body or mind work
- **d** medication given by a doctor

7 What type of drug is caffeine?

- **a** stimulant
- **b** depressant
- **c** hallucinogen
- **d** relaxant

8 Which of the following is **not** an over the counter (OTC) drug?

- **a** aspirin
- **b** paracetamol
- **c** cough syrup
- **d** antibiotic

9 Which of the following is **not** a sign of withdrawal symptoms?

- **a** sweating
- **b** happiness
- **c** fever
- **d** depression

10 Which of the following is an effect of a depressant drug?

- **a** temporary alertness and awareness
- **b** disorientation
- **c** reduction in brain activity
- **d** enhanced senses

11 Which of the following is **not** a method of transferring HIV from one person to another?

a sharing intravenous needles

b from an infected mother to her child at birth

c sitting on a public toilet seat

d having unprotected sexual intercourse with an infected person

12 What can inhibit the growth and replication of HIV?

a antiretroviral drugs **b** penicillin

c condoms **d** all of the above

13 Which of the following is used to kill bacteria?

a aspirin **b** alcohol

c antibiotic **d** caffeine

14 Which of these foods contains caffeine?

a tea **b** chocolate

c coffee **d** all of the above

15 Identify which of these is classed as a hard illegal drug.

a antibiotics **b** sleeping pills

c heroin **d** tobacco

16 What does STI stand for?

a semen timed insertion

b sexually transmitted infection

c standard testing instrument

d sexual time interval

17 Which STI is observed as painful blisters in the genitals that break out into sores?

a HIV/AIDS **b** herpes

c genital warts **d** all of the above

18 Which of these STIs is **not** caused by a virus?

a HIV **b** herpes

c genital warts **d** syphilis

19 What does AIDS stand for?

a Abstinence is Definitely Smart

b Acquired Immune Deficiency Syndrome

c Acquired Immunodeficiency Symptoms

d Adult Intelligence Data System

20 Which of these STIs can be treated with an antibiotic?

a herpes **b** HIV

c hepatitis **d** gonorrhoea

21 Which of these STIs has no known cure?

a chlamydia **b** HIV

c gonorrhoea **d** candidiasis

22 Which of these STIs has a symptom of painless sores around the genitals?

a syphilis **b** HIV

c gonorrhoea **d** herpes

23 Complete this sentence: A pregnant woman infected with the Zika virus is likely to have a baby born with…

a …Down's Syndrome **b** …microcephaly

c …blindness **d** …no limbs

24 Which of the following is **not** an illegal drug when purchased by an adult?

a alcohol **b** heroin

c ecstasy **d** cocaine

25 Identify the drug that is most likely to cause cirrhosis of the liver when consumed often and in excess.

a nicotine **b** alcohol

c caffeine **d** heroin

26 What is the addictive drug in tobacco?

a nicotine **b** alcohol

c caffeine **d** heroin

27 What is a *placebo* drug?

a an inactive substance used as a control in clinical trials

b a pill that contains a large dose of the drug

c an injection given with a large needle in the arm

d a capsule filled with air that is used in clinical trials

28 Why are mice often used during clinical trials?

a to kill unwanted mice

b to check for possible side effects

c to determine if mice will keep their fur after treatment with the drug

d to determine whether the drug is legal or illegal

29 Select the example of a drug used to enhance performance in sports.

a morphine **b** steroids

c marijuana **d** alcohol

30 Complete this sentence: Someone who has an uncontrollable habit of seeking for and using drugs is called a drug…

a …seeker

b …addict

c …injector

d …follower

Structured questions

Write your answers in the spaces provided.

1 STI stands for sexually transmitted infection.

a State **one** sure way in which the spread of STI can be prevented.

____

b What advice would you give to a person with multiple sex partners, to ensure they minimise the risk of catching an STI?

____

____

____

c What type of organism causes gonorrhoea? ______________________

d Give **two** symptoms that a male may observe if he has contracted gonorrhoea.

____

e State **two** possible effects of gonorrhoea on new-born babies if the mother is infected.

____

f How can gonorrhoea be treated?

____

g Complete this table.

STI	Causative agent	Two symptoms	Treatment	Effect if untreated
Syphilis				
Genital herpes				
Human Papilloma Virus				

2 Drugs can be classified into two main groups.

a Complete the chart by stating the two groups and giving **two** examples of drugs in each group.

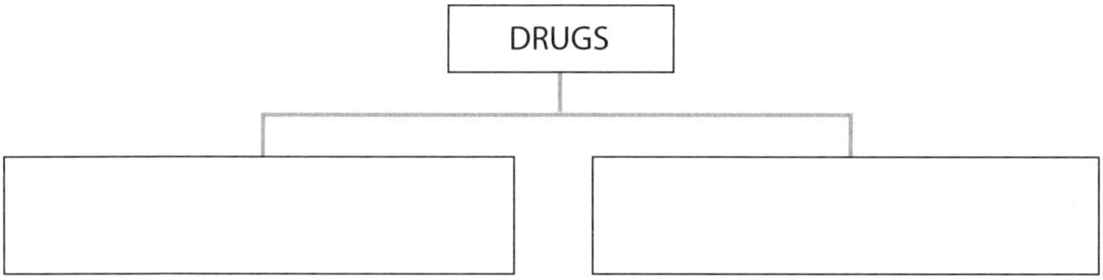

Examples:
1. ______________________
2. ______________________

Examples:
1. ______________________
2. ______________________

b For each drug you added to the chart, state its impact on the human body when used.

____

____

____

____

c Give **three** disadvantages of smoking cigarettes.

____

____

____

d A group of young people in your community attended a party. They all drank alcoholic drinks and left together; one of them drove the vehicle. Outline the dangers of this practice.

____

____

e You had a headache and the school nurse gave you paracetamol to ease the pain. What class of drug is paracetamol?

____

f State briefly how paracetamol works to relieve pain.

____

3 A teenager is addicted to heroin. He has been arrested for multiple accounts of robbery. His family members agree to enrol him in a drug rehabilitation programme.

a Briefly explain what a drug rehabilitation programme does.

____

____

b Research to find out **three** physical symptoms of someone addicted to heroin.

____

c Why might a heroin addict commit crimes such as robbery?

____

d A drug rehabilitation programme usually involves five basic steps. Complete the list by recording the missing steps.

1 __________ 2 __________ 3 __________

4 __________ 5 Monitoring

e Explain why *monitoring* is an important part of drug rehabilitation.

____

____

4 A drug company has designed a new drug which would stop heroin addicts from desiring heroin. During the pre-clinical phase, the drug was tested on male mice before the scientists conducted the study on human subjects.

a In your opinion, state **one** property that this drug should have in order to stop an addict from using heroin.

____

____

b Outline what happens during the pre-clinical research phase of a drug study.

____

____

c Identify the flaw in the pre-clinical phase described above.

____

d State why it would be a flaw in the study.

____

____

e Suggest an impact that this flaw may have on human studies.

____

____

Investigative comprehension

Read the comprehension passage and answer the questions that follow.

Drug use in the community

Varden lives in a community where drug use is rampant. There are lots of bars at which young people drink alcoholic drinks and socialise. Varden's parents have been very vigilant to ensure that he does not take drugs or drink alcohol, even though peer pressure is extreme.

Varden decided to conduct a study on drug use among the youth in his community. So, he travelled the street with the Pastor from his church one evening. People were happy to speak to Varden and provide the information he was after.

At the end of the investigation, Varden drew a Venn diagram to represent the data he collected:

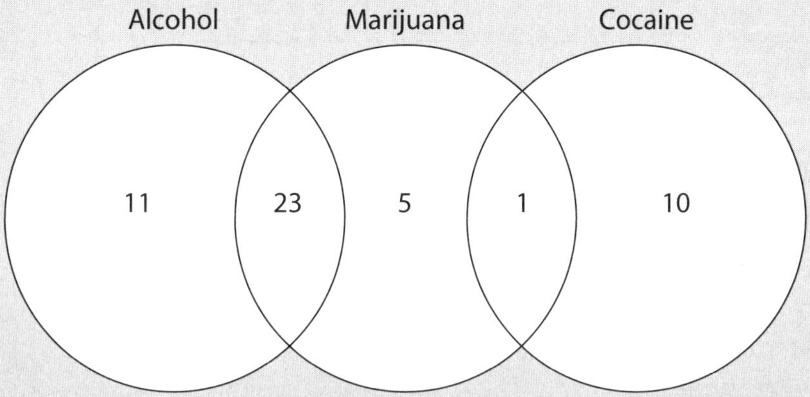

Varden discovered that, although alcohol use was common when socialising, some young people had become dependent and were now alcoholics. He also found out that the use of alcohol had a negative impact on the academic performance of some users.

1 In your opinion, explain why the young people in the community were willing to participate in Varden's survey.

____

____

2 What are the names of the **three** commonly used drugs in Varden's community?

____

3 How many young people participated in the survey? Show your working.

____

____

4 State the number of young people that used:

alcohol __________ cocaine __________

marijuana only __________ alcohol and marijuana __________

5 Which drug was the least used among the participants?

6 Give a reason for your answer to question **5**.

7 Is alcohol a medicinal drug or a recreational drug? Use information from the passage to give a reason for your answer.

8 Describe the effect that alcohol has on the human body and mind.

9 Explain the term *alcoholic*.

10 State **three** health effects that long term alcohol use has on the body.

11 Carry out some research to find out about the impact of drinking alcohol during pregnancy.

a **I** How does alcohol pass from a pregnant woman to her foetus?

II What effect does alcohol have on a foetus?

____

____

____

b I How does the alcohol pass from a lactating mother to her baby?

____

____

____

II What effect will alcohol have on the child of the lactating mother?

____

____

____

True or false?

State whether each statement is true or false.

1 AIDS is caused by a bacterium called HIV. ______

2 Nicotine is found in tea and coffee. ______

3 Someone who practices abstinence can become pregnant. ______

4 Having unprotected sex with a stranger is an irresponsible behaviour. ______

5 A sexually transmitted infection can be transferred by using a public toilet. ______

6 Gonorrhoea is caused by a bacterium. ______

7 Some strains of the Human Papilloma Virus (HPV) may cause cervical cancer. ______

8 All drugs are used for medicinal purposes. ______

9 A drug is misused if someone takes a larger dose than they are prescribed. ______

10 Caffeine is a depressant drug. ______

What am I?

Write the name of who or what the statement refers to.

1 Common drug found in coffee and tea. ______

2 The virus that causes AIDS. ______

3 STI that gives a yellow pus-like discharge from the genitals. ______

4 A type of drug that increases the activity of the brain. ______

5 Yeast infection of the vagina. ______

6 Virus that can cause microcephaly in newborns. ______

7 Chemical that changes the way that the body and mind works. ______

8 Drug found in beer, wine and rum. ______

Matching

Draw lines to connect the drug rehabilitation stages to their correct descriptions.

Drug rehabilitation stages	Description
detoxification	treating withdrawal symptoms
counselling	dealing with mental health issues such as depression
medication	helping someone to change their behaviours and habits towards the use of the drug
evaluation/treatment	meeting to reduce the risk of relapse into drug use
monitoring	getting rid of the drug from the body

Fill in the blanks

Complete the passage using the words below. Some words can be used once, more than once or not at all.

sick cocaine vomiting disease drug

fevers dependence addicted withdrawal addict addiction misuse

Drug addiction is a chronic ____________________. A person who has a severe ____________________ on drugs is called a drug ____________________.
A psychological dependence occurs when the body does not need the ____________________ but the mind thinks that it does. In some cases, the body will no longer work properly unless the drug is taken.

Heroin and ____________________ are examples of illegal drugs that cause users to develop an ____________________ to them very quickly, but people can become addicted to any drug if they ____________________ them.

When someone becomes ____________________ to a drug, they may feel ____________________ if they attempt to stop using it.

These effects are called ____________________. The symptoms of ____________________ may cause a person to experience ____________________, profuse sweating, and ____________________.

Developing a scientific mind

1 Write a rap or poem about the life changing impact that contracting HIV/AIDS would have on someone's life.

Crossword puzzle

Across

1. A sexually transmitted infection (STI) caused by the Human Immunodeficiency Virus (HIV).
3. The type of infections that invade the body when its immune system is depressed.
5. The drug found in wines and beers.
6. From the time you reach puberty you may begin to have sensual sensations and have moments of ___.
7. A drug that reduces the sense of pain and induces relaxation.
9. Yeast infection.
11. A drug found in coffee.
13. Sexually transmitted infection.
15. STI causing a yellow pus-like discharge from the genitals.
16. The use of a banned drug.
17. The only sexual behaviour with no risk of contracting an STI.

Down

2. An STI caused by a bacterium and characterised by the presence of small painless sores around the genitals.
4. When a drug is used for another purpose than that for which is intended.
6. A hormone that triggers a sense of fright or surprise and causes the heart to race.
8. The addictive substance in tobacco.
10. A drug that increases brain activity and alertness.
12. A virus that can be transferred sexually or by a mosquito.
14. A chemical substance that affects the way the body and mind works.

UNIT 8 Climate change

Multiple choice questions

Circle the letter that *best* corresponds to the answer of your choice.

1 Regular weather patterns experienced throughout the year are known as what?

a seasons **b** climate
c hurricane **d** precipitation

2 How many seasons does Jamaica have?

a one **b** two **c** three **d** four

3 At what time of year does the rainy season occur in Jamaica?

a May to June
b October
c September to November
d May to June and September to November

4 Which of these statements best describe(s) effects of climate change?

a winters get colder
b increased flooding in some regions
c melting of the ice caps and glaciers
d all of the above

5 Which of the following is **not** a greenhouse gas?

a carbon dioxide
b hydrofluorocarbons
c oxygen
d methane

6 Identify the example(s) of how human activity that increases greenhouse gas emissions.

a rearing of cattle **b** bush fires
c burning fuels **d** all of the above

7 What does the accumulation of greenhouse gases in the atmosphere contribute to?

a the green gas effect **b** global warming
c the gas age **d** global dimming

8 Which human activity is most likely to help reduce the rate of global warming?

a burning garbage
b using wind or solar energy
c washing small loads of clothing instead of full loads
d using electrical appliances as often as possible

9 Complete this sentence: The solar energy which reaches Earth's surface will…

a …warm the Earth's surface
b …cause droughts in Africa
c …cause earthquakes to happen
d …transmit magnetic signals to Earth

10 Which of these is **not** an effect of climate change?

- **a** rising sea levels
- **b** flooding of coastal lines
- **c** extreme weather patterns
- **d** expanding glaciers

11 Which of these conditions would contribute to the greenhouse effect?

- **a** excess nitrogen in the atmosphere
- **b** excess carbon dioxide in the atmosphere
- **c** heat from cooking fires
- **d** none of the above

12 Which of these is a source of carbon dioxide?

- **a** campfires
- **b** respiration
- **c** erupting volcanoes
- **d** all of the above

13 Which of these gases is most likely to deplete the ozone?

- **a** chlorofluorocarbons
- **b** carbon dioxide
- **c** sulphur dioxide
- **d** carbon monoxide

14 Which gas prevents haemoglobin from carrying oxygen around the body?

- **a** oxygen
- **b** carbon dioxide
- **c** sulphur dioxide
- **d** carbon monoxide

15 Complete this sentence: Global dimming is caused by…

- **a** …clouds blocking the sunlight
- **b** …the accumulation of particles in the atmosphere that block the sunlight
- **c** …dimming of the Sun, reducing the amount of light reaching Earth
- **d** …greenhouse gases accumulating in the atmosphere

16 What is *smog*?

- **a** a mixture of greenhouse gases
- **b** carbon monoxide
- **c** polluted fog
- **d** another term used for fog

17 Identify the statement that best describes a function of mangroves.

- **a** prevent small fish from coming too close to shore
- **b** protect the coastline by preventing erosion
- **c** prevent fish from laying eggs close to human habitats
- **d** attract tourists

18 What is a long, dry season called?

- **a** desert
- **b** drought
- **c** heatstroke
- **d** summer

19 Which of the following statements are possible future results of the greenhouse effect?

- **a** air temperature will rise
- **b** polar ice caps will melt
- **c** changes in rainfall patterns
- **d** all of the above

20 Which of the following is a sign of climate change in Jamaica?

- **a** endemic species of plants are thriving
- **b** forests and woodlands are flourishing and expanding
- **c** plants have an excess of raw materials needed for photosynthesis
- **d** habitats are lost and there is limited food available for many organisms

21 This is an image of the Jamaican giant swallowtail butterfly. What is the most likely effect of climate change on this organism?

- **a** it will grow larger
- **b** it will change its migration patterns
- **c** it will experience more predation
- **d** it will change its reproductive cycle

22 Complete this sentence: An increase in ocean temperature will…

- **a** …destroy coral reefs
- **b** …increase the rate of reproduction of marine organisms
- **c** …sustain the coral reef
- **d** …make more organisms retreat to the coral reef as a habitat

23 Complete this sentence: Turtle nests are found in…

- **a** deep seas
- **b** sand on beaches
- **c** coral reefs
- **d** land swamps

24 What factor affects the gender (male or female) of a turtle?

- **a** location of the nest
- **b** length of daylight hours in a day
- **c** amount of rain when eggs are laid
- **d** temperature of the sand in which eggs are laid

25 Which type of light bulb will help to reduce the impact of climate change?

- **a** incandescent
- **b** compact fluorescent
- **c** halogen
- **d** none of the above

26 Which of the following energy sources will **not** reduce the impact of climate change?

- **a** charcoal
- **b** wind
- **c** solar
- **d** geothermal

27 When does the hurricane season occur in Jamaica?

- **a** January to July
- **b** July to October
- **c** June to July
- **d** June to November

28 Which of the following is **not** a source of methane?

- **a** volcanic eruptions
- **b** cattle rearing
- **c** deforestation
- **d** decomposition of biomass

29 What chemical is used to test for carbon dioxide in the laboratory?

- **a** lime juice
- **b** vinegar
- **c** lime water
- **d** baking soda

30 What is the predicted average temperature rise of the Earth's surface temperature by the year 2100?

- **a** 0.99 °C
- **b** 0.5 °C
- **c** 1.5 °C
- **d** 1.0 °C

Structured questions

Write your answers in the spaces provided.

1 Study the bar chart and answer the questions that follow.

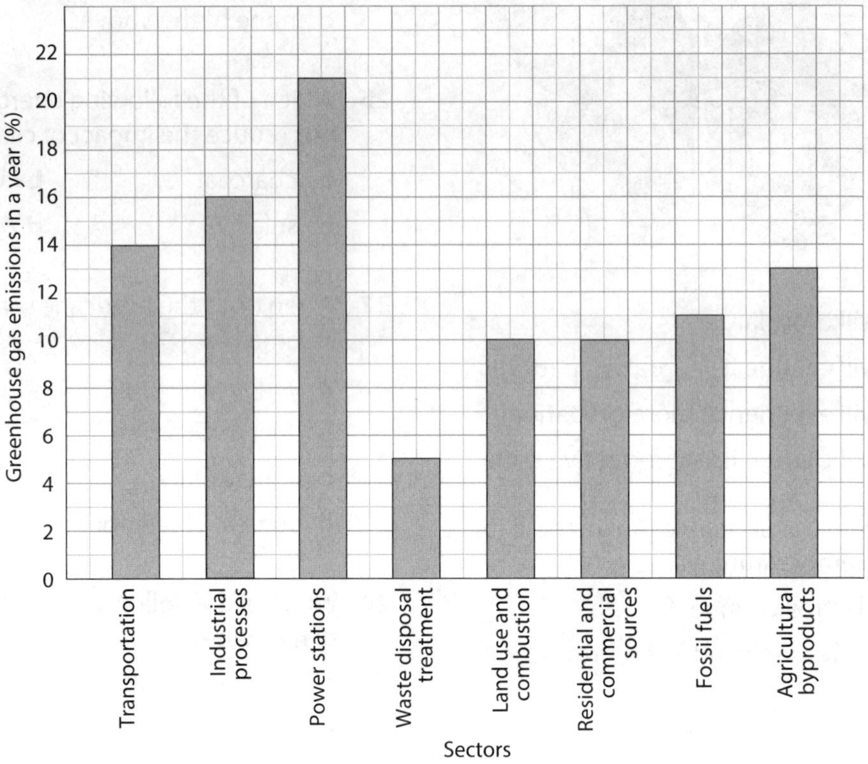

a Give the graph a suitable title.

____

b Use the information on the graph to complete this table.

Sectors	Greenhouse gas emissions in a year (%)
Transportation	
Industrial processes	
Power stations	
Waste disposal treatment	
Land use and combustion	10
Residential and commercial sources	10
Fossil fuels	
Agricultural by-products	

c According to the graph, which human activity contributes the most greenhouse gas emissions?

____

d Describe how agriculture may contribute to the production of greenhouse gases.

____

____

____

e Which **three** sectors combined will account for 50% of the annual greenhouse gas emissions?

____

f Describe **two** ways in which humans can reduce the amount of greenhouse gases emitted from residential sources.

____

____

____

2 Carbon dioxide is a greenhouse gas.

a Find out the chemical formula of carbon dioxide.

____

b Find out the names of the elements that make up carbon dioxide.

____

c Name **three** sources of carbon dioxide.

____

____

____

d What is the name of the chemical used to test for carbon dioxide in the laboratory, and what observation shows a positive result?

____

e Name **two** chemicals used in the home which can be reacted to produce carbon dioxide gas.

____

f Look at this apparatus used to test for carbon dioxide.

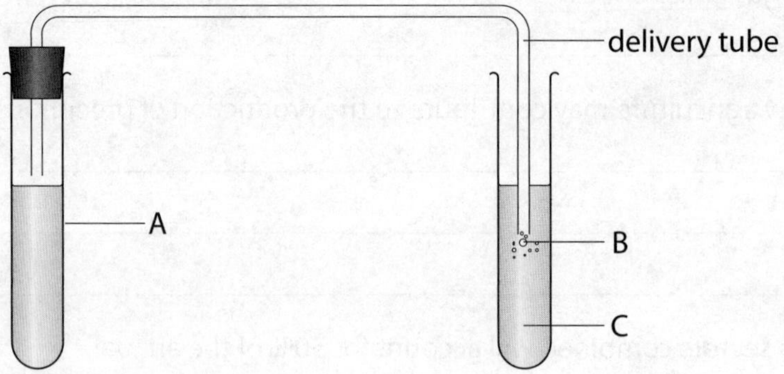

I Label elements A to C.

A ______________________________ and ______________________________

B ______________________________ C ______________________________

II What is the function of the delivery tube?

____

____

g Explain how carbon dioxide contributes to global warming.

____

____

____

h State **one** method of removing carbon dioxide from the environment.

____

____

3 There are other pollutant gases in the atmosphere that are not greenhouse gases. Name **two** of these gases and state their impact on the environment.

a Pollutant gas: ______________________________

Effect on the environment:

____

____

b Pollutant gas: ______________________________

Effect on the environment:

____

____

4 Read this statement:

'Global warming keeps the Earth's surface warm and habitable for all living organisms, including humans.'

a Do you agree with the statement? Support your answer with factual arguments.

____

____

____

____

____

b State **three** ways in which climate change has impacted Jamaica.

____

____

____

____

c State **one** way in which climate change has impacted the following sectors in Jamaica.

Tourism industry:

____

____

Agriculture:

____

____

d Climate change seems to affect how animals reproduce. Give **one** example of how climate change has affected the reproduction of an animal.

____

____

____

Investigative comprehension

Read the comprehension passage and answer the questions that follow.

Reducing the effects of climate change

Renalta is a Grade 7 student. In class, she learned that human activity has been the largest contributor of greenhouse gases. Activities such as deforestation, combustion (burning), mining, and overall industrialisation has had a major impact on increasing the volume of greenhouse gases in the atmosphere. Deforestation involves the cutting down of trees and contributes to global warming because trees provide the only method of removing carbon dioxide from the atmosphere by the process of photosynthesis. Without trees, carbon dioxide accumulates in the atmosphere, increasing the greenhouse effect.

After learning about greenhouse gases, Renalta decided to actively promote strategies to reduce the effects of climate change. She lives in a very small community – all the students in her class live no more than a 15 minute walk from school.

Renalta conducted a survey to find out how the students in her class traveled to school: five students walk to school, eight are driven in a family vehicle and 12 use a taxi.

After collecting the data, Renalta made some suggestions to her classmates so they could help reduce the impact of climate change.

1 Explain why Renalta wanted to reduce the effect of climate change after learning about greenhouse gases.

____

____

2 Explain the link between modern lifestyles and global warming.

____

____

____

3 a Tabulate the data collected by Renalta.

Mode of transport	Number of students

b Draw a bar chart to illustrate the data collected.

c Calculate the percentage of students that walk to school. Show your working.

d Suggest what information Renalta should share with her classmates to persuade them to reduce the effects of climate change. Give a reason for your answer.

e List **three** other strategies Renalta and her classmates could adopt to reduce the effects of climate change.

6 Carry out some research to answer the following questions.

a Is Jamaica above or below sea level? Provide some data about its altitude.

b Indicate whether rising sea levels will affect Jamaica more or less than the Netherlands.

c Using the engineering design process, devise an invention that might help those affected by flooding. Describe your invention and explain how it would work.

True or false?

State whether each statement is true or false.

1 Global warming is caused only by natural factors. ____________

2 Hurricanes do not affect Jamaica. ____________

3 Climate change can lead to extreme flooding and drought in different regions on Earth. ____________

4 Carbon dioxide is a greenhouse gas. ____________

5 Carbon monoxide, when inhaled, can be fatal for humans. ____________

6 Sulphur dioxide is important for purifying the air. ____________

7 Smog is formed when greenhouse gases block the light from the Sun. ____________

8 Climate change may lead to some organisms migrating in search of food and a place to live. ____________

9 An increase in the Earth's temperature will cause plants to grow rapidly. ____________

10 The temperature of a turtle's nest affects the gender of its babies when hatched. ____________

What am I?

Write the name of who or what the statement refers to.

1 A potent greenhouse gas. ____________

2 An atmospheric pollutant that depletes the ozone layer. ____________

3 Harmful substances that destroy the environment. ____________

4 The most abundant greenhouse gas. ____________

5 Different weather conditions that occur at predictable times of year; Jamaica is said to have two of these. ____________

6 Caused by long periods without rainfall. ____________

7 Result of drastic, and sometimes devastating, changes in weather patterns all year round. ____________

8 Causes reduction in the coastline and the sea reclaiming land around the island. ____________

Matching

Use this table to label the diagram, A–F.

A	Some of the radiation from the Sun is reflected back into space	**B**	The Sun's energy heats the Earth's surface
C	Greenhouse gases trap the heat energy by radiating it back to the Earth, causing the Earth's atmosphere to become warmer	**D**	Some of the Sun's radiation passes through the earth's atmosphere
E	Radiation from the Sun	**F**	A layer of greenhouse gases in the atmosphere

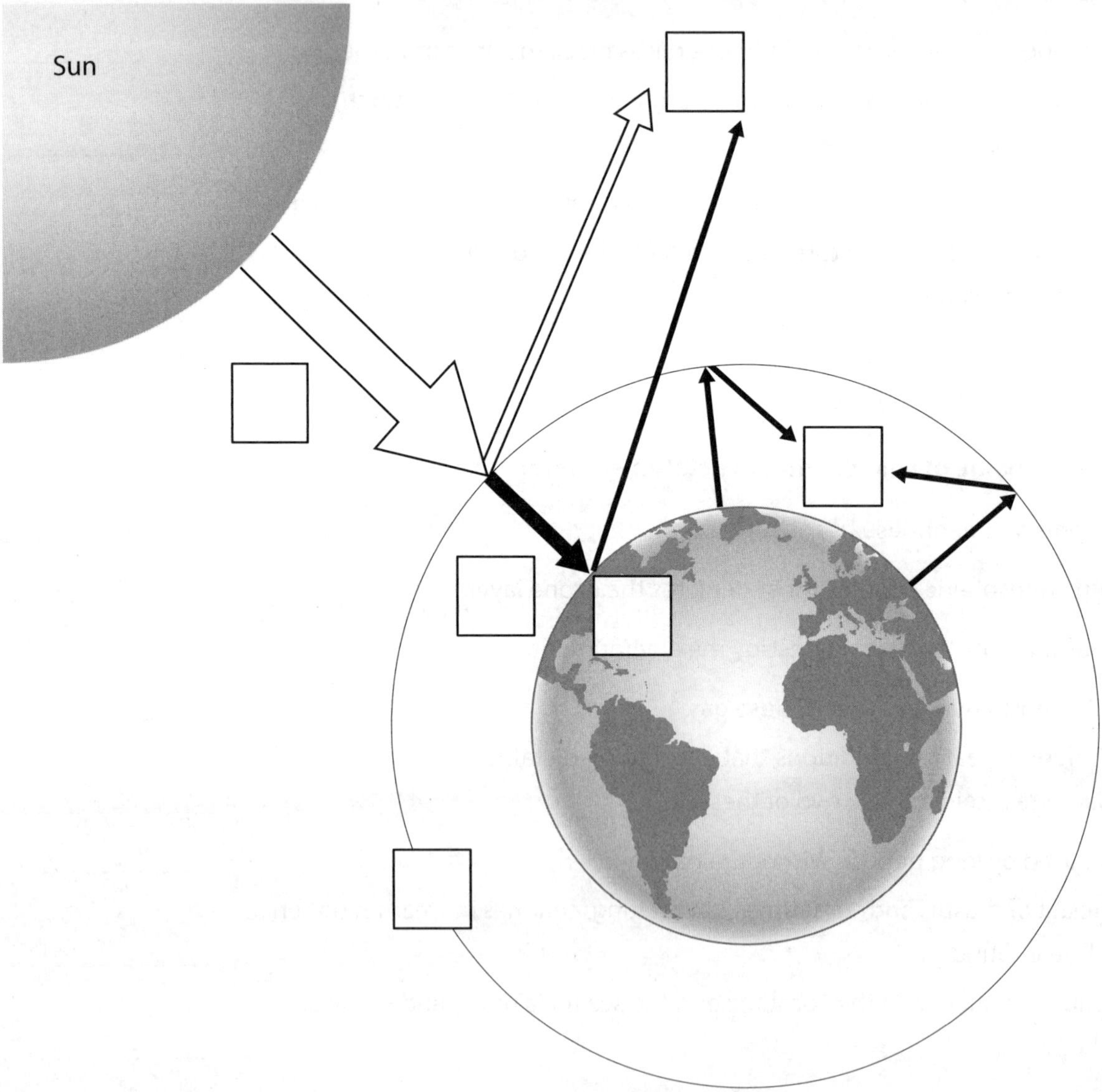

Fill in the blanks

Complete the passage using the words below. Some words can be used once, more than once or not at all.

temperature hurricanes change greenhouse normal reflected
two flooding glaciers methane decrease Caribbean dioxide tropical
increase rainy patterns atmosphere Earth wildfires climate dry

Jamaica has a ______________________ climate, therefore it has two seasons: the ______________________ season and the ______________________ season.

In addition, at a specific time each year, the islands of the Caribbean are prone to ______________________, which can have a devastating impact on the places they pass over.

Any drastic change from the normal weather ______________________ within a year could be an effect of climate change.

Climate change is mainly caused by an ______________________ in the temperature of the Earth caused by the ______________________ effect. This effect results from the build-up of gases, such as ______________________ ______________________, ______________________ and nitrous oxide. These gases form a layer in the ______________________ which allows the heat energy in but prevents it from being reflected back into space.

Climate change can cause problems such as drought, ______________________, flooding and rising sea levels due to melting glaciers.

Developing a scientific mind

1 Write an article for your local newspaper, describing **three** effects of global warming in Jamaica. Make sure your article looks like it comes from a newspaper. You can use the space below and draw pictures or glue in photos. If available, you can use computer software to design and present your article.

Remember to give your article a catchy headline and make sure you use facts that apply to Jamaica.

Double puzzle

Unscramble each of the vocabulary terms, then take the letters that appear in the circles and unscramble them for the final vocabulary term.

TILMACE HEGCNA

GEERONHUES SAG

HEEGUNREOS FECTEF

BOANCR EDOIXID

TOILONPUL

LALBOG DMGMNII

RUGOTHD

RINSOEO

DAONIAPATT

NICRASVOTNEO

The final vocabulary word is:

W